The Copyright Guide

A Friendly Handbook for Protecting and Profiting from Copyrights

by Lee Wilson

Allworth Press
NEW YORK

Published by Allworth Press
an imprint of Allworth Communications, Inc.
10 East 23rd Street
New York, NY 10010

Cover design by Douglas Design Associates, New York, NY
Book design by Sharp Des!gns, Holt, MI

ISBN: 1-880559-43-9

Library of Congress Catalog Card Number: 95-83005

Printed in Canada

This book is dedicated to my parents, Jerry and Miriam Wilson. They don't know much about copyrights, but they allowed me to spend half my childhood sitting in a tree or a quiet corner or the back seat of our '57 Chevy with a book. I read in the bathtub and during meals and when I was supposed to be doing chores. I even read at parties and on visits to our many relatives. They never said a word to stop me, except, at night, "It's late! Turn off the light!" I have been very fortunate in my choice of parents, and I am grateful to them for a happy childhood, which is a head start on a happy life.

Contents

Introduction

THIS BOOK IS WRITTEN for everyone who creates, acquires, or exploits copyrights. Copyright owners constitute an increasingly large segment of our society. This group includes painters; illustrators; photographers; filmmakers; sculptors; graphic designers; industrial designers; jewelry designers; textile designers; journalists; novelists; poets; screenwriters; playwrights; technical writers; copywriters; students; scholars; editors; researchers; songwriters; composers; record producers; recording artists; choreographers; computer software designers; and television and movie directors and producers; as well as newspaper, book, and magazine publishers; educational institutions; radio and television broadcasters; toy manufacturers; music publishers; record companies; movie studios; museums and art collectors; software companies; advertising agencies; poster companies; photo archives and stock photo houses; theatrical producers; dance companies; pop music tour promoters; and manufacturers of all sorts of consumer products. In fact, unless you engage solely in a profession or occupation that produces and sells only tangible products, you must know, in today's world, something about the most common sort of intangible property—copyrights.

For anyone whose livelihood or avocation is centered in one of the U.S. information industries, copyrights and the exploitation of copyrights are a basic fact of life. A good case could be made for the premise that no one in America escapes the effect of copyrights. There may be no spot in your house or school or office where you are not surrounded by copyrights. The copy and illustrations on the box your breakfast cereal comes in are copyrighted. Every book in your school locker, except for pre-twentieth-century works, is copyrighted. The professional journals or trade publications at your office are copyrighted, as is every memorandum, letter, report, proposal, or other document you produce on the job. Copyrights float through the air as radio and television broadcasts and arrive in the mail as magazines and newspapers and show up in shopping bags as compact disks and bestseller novels and video games for the kids.

Of course, this proliferation of expression may be a mixed blessing. We are inundated by our own communications. Toddlers who can't read know the names of all the Power Rangers and the Teenage Mutant Ninja Turtles. College students who can't remember the date of the Norman Conquest can recite dialogue from reruns of *The Brady Bunch.* Their grandmothers can recall the convolutions of plot from television soap operas for the last twenty-five years. And aging baby boomers can sing every word of popular songs from their youth, almost on key.

We have an embarrassment of riches. And we share our wealth— our principal export is American popular culture. Whether this is good or bad has yet to be seen, but it is a given that, in the global village, Americans are center stage.

This is mostly because the United States is unique in its cultural affection for and legal protection of free expression. We forget that we are the only nation that has the First Amendment. Many other nations impose more restrictions on what their citizens can say and write and publish than we do. In fact, throughout history, during numerous periods and in various places, you could be imprisoned or killed simply for saying or writing the wrong thing; unfortunately, this is still the case in some places.

But not in America. The rebels and mavericks who sailed across the oceans in wooden boats to settle in what became the United States knew the value of free thought and free speech. They came here seeking both. Aside from the stubborn individualism that still characterizes Americans, they gave us the right to think what we want and say what we think.

But even before the enactment of the First Amendment, the men who wrote our Constitution acted to ensure the production of the works of art and intellect necessary to create and promote culture and learning in our infant nation. In Article 1, Section 8, Clause 8 of the main body of the original, unamended, Constitution, they gave Congress the power "to Promote the Progress of Science and useful Arts, by securing, for limited Times to Authors and Inventors, the exclusive Right to their respective Writings and Discoveries." Congress carried out this mandate by passing the first U.S. copyright statute in 1790. (And by enacting a succession of patent statutes.) You may think from reading the language of the Constitution that only authors of books are protected by copyright law. That is not the case.

Historically, American copyright law has interpreted broadly the "writings" granted constitutional protection. At the time of the enactment of the first copyright statute, only "maps, charts, and books" were protected. During the two centuries since, U.S. copyright statutes (there have been several) and court decisions have extended copyright protection to new subjects of copyright as previously non-existent classes of works emerged, needing protection. U.S. copyright statutes successively embraced, among other new technologies, photography, motion pictures, and sound recordings.

This system of enumerating the classes of "writings" protected by copyright worked well enough until it became obvious that technology would create new methods of expression faster than the courts and lawmakers could amend copyright statutes to include emerging technologies within the scope of copyright protection. The present U.S. copyright statute abandons the effort to enumerate every class of work protected by copyright and simply states that "copyright protection subsists . . . in original works of authorship fixed in any tangible medium of expression, now known or later developed, from which they can be perceived, reproduced, or otherwise communicated, either directly or with the aid of a machine or device." This language allows copyright to expand automatically to extend protection to new forms of expression. This is fortunate, because the revolution in communications that has characterized the last half-century shows no sign of abating. Indeed, it may be reaching warp speed.

By recognizing property rights in creative works and awarding ownership of those rights to the creators of the works, our copyright statute encourages expression in every art form and medium. It balances the interests of creators against those of the public. Creators reap the profits from their works for the duration of copyright protection by limiting access to creative works to those who pay for the privilege of using them. The public immediately enjoys controlled access to the works artists, writers, and composers create and, eventually, those works become public property, available for use by anyone. This is precisely what the founding fathers had in mind; James Madison cited copyright as an instance in which the "public good fully coincides . . . with the claims of individuals."

So, the United States gives its citizens the right to say almost anything at all and rewards that expression, whether meritorious or mundane, by bestowing upon it a copyright. But what, exactly, is a copyright? A copyright is a set of rights that the federal copyright statute grants to the creators of literary, musical, dramatic, choreographic, pictorial, graphic, sculptural, and audiovisual works and sound recordings. Copyright law rewards creators by granting them the exclusive right to exploit and control their creations. With few narrow exceptions, only the person who created the copyrighted work or someone to whom he or she has sold the copyright in the work or given permission to use the work is legally permitted to reproduce the work, to prepare alternate or "derivative" versions of the work, to distribute and sell copies of the work, and to perform or display the work publicly. Any unauthorized exercise of any of these rights is called "copyright infringement" and is actionable in federal court.

But this is only the beginning of the story. The rest follows in what I hope is a logical progression. I have practiced intellectual-property law for nearly one-third of my life, but I still find the concept of copyright and all the elaborate structures that our world community has erected around it fascinating. The law says that a copyright is a set of exclusive rights that belong, in most instances, to the person who creates the copyrighted work. That's true, but what copyrights really are is magic. There's something wonderful in the fact that in a mass culture like ours, where individual voices are obscured by the noise of the rat race, you can create, all alone and out of thin air and your own brain, something that pays the rent.

I hope you find copyrights as interesting as I do. They are one of the last means by which an individual person, unaffiliated with any large organization or institution, can change people's minds, lift their spirits, and feed their souls. Where's your pencil?

LEE WILSON
Nashville, Tennessee

CHAPTER 1

Copyright Protection

BEFORE YOU CAN begin to understand copyright—that invisible but powerful and infinitely expandable concept that governs so many of our dealings with each other—you must first learn what it is not. Two of the things that copyright is not are trademarks and patents. The three forms of intellectual property are more like cousins than triplets, but lots of people, even lawyers and judges, confuse them.

Copyrights Compared to Trademarks and Patents

Although all three protect products of the human imagination, copyrights, trademarks, and patents are distinct but complementary sorts of intellectual property. Each is governed by a different federal law. The U.S. patent statute originates in the same provision of the Constitution that gives rise to our copyright statute. Our federal trademark statute originates in the "commerce clause" of the Constitution, which gives Congress the power to regulate interstate commerce. Only our federal government regulates copyrights;

copyright registrations are granted by the Copyright Office, which is a department of the Library of Congress. Similarly, only the federal government can grant a patent. However, although the federal government grants trademark registrations, so do all fifty states.

Copyrights

Since January 1, 1978, in the United States, a copyright is created whenever a creator "fixes" in tangible form a work for which copyright protection is available. Under most circumstances, a copyright will endure until fifty years after the death of the creator of the copyrighted work; after copyright protection expires a work is said to have fallen into the "public domain" and anyone is free to use it. Registration of a copyright enhances the rights that a creator automatically gains by the act of creation, but it is not necessary for copyright protection. The chief limitation on the rights of copyright owners is that copyright protects only particular *expressions* of ideas rather than the ideas themselves. This means that several people can create copyrightable works based on the same idea; in fact, there is no infringement no matter how similar one work is to another unless one creator copied another's work.

Trademarks

Trademarks are words or symbols that identify products or services to consumers. Unlike a copyright, in which the creator has protectable rights from the inception of the copyrighted work, rights in a trademark accrue only by use of the trademark in commerce; they then belong to the company that applies the mark to its products, rather than to the person who came up with the name or designed the logo that becomes the trademark. Roughly speaking, a company gains rights in a trademark in direct proportion to the geographic scope and duration of its use of the mark; ordinarily, the company that first uses a mark gains rights in that mark superior to any other company that later uses it for the same product or services. Unauthorized use of a trademark is "trademark infringement."

As is the case with copyrights, registration enhances rights in trademarks but does not create them. It is generally easy to register a mark within a state, but federal trademark registration, which confers much greater benefits, is more difficult to obtain. Trademark rights last indefinitely; as long as a mark is used in commerce, its owners have protectable rights in it.

(For more information about trademarks, see the forthcoming book by Lee Wilson, *The Trademark Guide,* to be published by Allworth Press, New York.)

Patents

The word "patent" is used ordinarily to designate the rights granted by the federal government to the originator of a physical invention or industrial or technical process (a "utility patent"), or an ornamental design for an "article of manufacture" (a "design patent"). Utility patents last seventeen years, design patents fourteen years.

A patent holder earns the exclusive right to make, use, and sell the invention for which the patent was granted. Any unauthorized manufacture, use, or sale of the patented invention within this country during the term of the patent is infringement.

(For more information about patents, see the forthcoming book by Carl W. Battle, *The Patent Guide,* to be published by Allworth Press, New York.)

Requirements for Copyright Protection

Under the U.S. copyright statute, a work must satisfy three conditions to qualify for copyright protection. All three of these requirements must be met in order for the work to come under the copyright umbrella. The three statutory prerequisites for protection are: (1) the work must be "original" in the sense that it cannot have been copied from another work; (2) the work must embody some "expression" of the author, rather than consisting only of an idea or ideas; and (3) the work must be "fixed" in some tangible medium of expression.

Originality

The originality condition for protection leads to the apparent anomaly that two works identical to each other may be equally eligible for copyright protection. So long as neither of the two works was copied from the other, each is considered "original." In the sense it is used in the copyright statute, "originality" means simply that a work was not copied from another work, rather than that the work is unique or unusual. Judge Learned Hand, a jurist who decided many copyright cases, summarized the originality requirement with a famous hypothetical example: "[I]f by some magic a man who had never known it were to compose anew Keats's *Ode on a Grecian Urn,* he would be an 'author,' and, if he copyrighted it, others might not copy the poem, though they might of course copy Keats's." For copyright purposes, the similarities between two works are immaterial, so long as they do not result from copying.

Expression

The current copyright statute restates the accepted rule, often enunciated in copyright decisions, that copyright subsists only in the expression embodied in a work and not in the underlying ideas upon which the work is based. The statute says: "In no case does copyright protection for an original work of authorship extend to any idea, procedure, process, system, method of operation, concept, principle, or discovery, regardless of the form in which it is described, explained, illustrated, or embodied in such work." This rule plays an important role in copyright infringement cases, because a judge must often determine whether the defendant has taken protected expression from the plaintiff or merely "borrowed" an unprotectable idea (or "procedure, process, system," etc.).

Fixation

The U.S. copyright statute protects works eligible for protection only when they are "fixed in any tangible medium of expression, now known or later developed, from which they can be perceived, reproduced, or otherwise communicated, either directly or with the aid of a machine or device." The statute deems a work fixed in a tangible medium of expression "when its embodiment in a copy or phonorecord, by or under the authority of the author, is sufficiently permanent or stable to permit it to be perceived, reproduced, or otherwise communicated for a period of more than transitory duration."

This third requirement for copyright protection sometimes surprises people, who may not realize, for instance, that a new song performed at an open mike "writers' night" or a dance routine presented in a talent show, although it is both original and contains a high proportion of protectable expression, is not protected by copyright until it is "fixed" within the definition of the copyright statute and can be legally copied, word for word or move for move, by anyone who witnesses its performance. A song can be "fixed" by recording any intelligible version of its music and lyrics on a cassette or by reducing its melody to written musical notation that also includes its lyrics. Any piece of choreography can be "fixed" by videotaping it in sufficient detail to record the movements of the dancers or by use of a written system of choreographic notation such as Labanotation.

What Is Protected

Most people realize that copyright protects works of art like poems and short stories, photographs, paintings and drawings, and musical compositions. It may be less obvious that copyright also protects more mundane forms of expression, including such diverse materials as advertising copy, instruction manuals, brochures, logo designs, computer programs, term papers, home movies, cartoon strips, and advertising jingles. Artistic merit has nothing to do with whether a work is protectable by copyright; in fact, the most routine business letter and the most inexpertly executed child's drawing are just as entitled to protection under our copyright statute as the bestselling novels, hit songs, and blockbuster movies.

However, copyright does not protect every product of the imagination, no matter how many brain cells were expended in its creation. In fact, any discussion of copyright protection must be premised on an understanding of what copyright *does not* protect.

Idea Versus Expression

It is such an important principle of copyright law that it bears repeating: copyright protects only particular *expressions* of ideas, not the ideas themselves. This means, of course, that if the guy sitting behind you on the bus looks over your shoulder and sees, comprehends, and remembers your sketches for a necklace formed of links cast in the shape of sunflowers, he is legally free to create his own sunflower necklace so long as it isn't a copy of yours. It may be *unethical* for him to steal your idea, but it's neither illegal nor actionable in court. Although this may seem unjust, if you think about it, it's logical. Our Constitution empowered Congress to pass a copyright statute granting the creators among us property rights in the products of their imaginations so that American society could gain the benefit of their creations. Because ideas are the building blocks for creations of any sort, and because one idea may lead to thousands of expressions of that idea, granting control over an idea to any one person would have the effect of severely limiting creative expression; no one else would be able to use the idea as the basis for a new creation.

Therefore, copyright protects only your particular *expression* of an idea, *not* the idea itself. Similarly, copyright protection is denied to procedures, processes, systems, methods of operation, concepts, principles, or discoveries because these products of the imagination are really all particular varieties of ideas.

This means that your *idea* of printing grocery coupons right on the brown paper bags used in your supermarket can be copied by anyone, even a competing grocery store, although the particular expression of your idea—your copy and artwork for the bags and the advertisements publicizing the promotion—may not.

And your *system* of giving your customers double the face-value discount of any coupon if they use it to buy two product items at the same time is not protectable by your copyright in your coupon-promotion materials and can be employed at any time by anyone, without your permission.

Further, if you print recipes on your grocery bags in addition to discount coupons, you cannot, of course, stop anyone from using the *method* outlined in the "Low-Fat Meatloaf" recipe to create a low-fat meatloaf. Nor can you stop anyone, even a competitor, from employing your *concept* of using a low-fat meatloaf recipe to sell the food products used in the recipe or from employing the marketing *principle* behind your promotion—that food shoppers are likely to purchase particular brands of food products that are specified by name in an interesting recipe. And even though you were the first person in the universe to come up with a technique for diminishing the fat content of the finished dish, once you disclose your *discovery* to the public, you can't stop anyone from recounting it to anyone else.

You can't even stop anyone from using the *information* outlined in your meatloaf recipe to create his or her own recipe for low-fat meatloaf. (See the discussion of functional works below.)

Unprotectable Elements

There are a few categories of products of the imagination that are too close to being merely unembellished ideas for copyright protection to apply. In other words, these categories of "creations" lack sufficient expression to be granted copyright protection. There are several commonly occurring unprotectable elements of various sorts of works from which the copyright statute or courts have withheld protection. These include:

- literary plots, situations, locales or settings;
- *scènes à faire,* which are stock literary themes that dictate the incidents used by an author to express them;
- literary characters, to the extent that they are "types" rather than original expressions of an author, as opposed to pictorial characters, the visual representation of which adds considerable protectable expression to the characters;
- titles of books, stories, poems, songs, movies, etc., which have been uniformly held by courts not to be protected by copyright (although a title may gain protection under the law of unfair competition if it becomes well-known and associated in the public mind with one author);
- short phrases and slogans, to the extent that they lack expressive content, the determination of which is aided by the length of the phrase or slogan, very short phrases and slogans being

more likely to constitute the equivalent of an unprotectable idea than long phrases or slogans;

- the rhythm or structure of musical works;
- themes expressed by song lyrics;
- short musical phrases;
- arrangements of musical compositions, unless an arrangement of a musical composition really amounts to an alternate version of the composition, in which case the arrangement infringes the underlying composition unless it was written with the permission of the owner of copyright in that composition (The exception to this is an arrangement of a public domain song. Since you can use a public domain composition any way you want, it's legal to make a detailed arrangement of such a song, and the arrangement is protectable.);
- social dance steps and simple routines, which are not copyrightable as choreographic works because they are the common property of the culture that enjoys them;
- uses of color, perspective, geometric shapes, and standard arrangements dictated by aesthetic convention in works of the visual arts (however, an artist's *arrangement* of these elements may be protectable expression);
- jewelry designs that merely mimic the structures of nature, such as a jeweled pin that accurately replicates the form of a honeybee;
- names of products, services, or businesses (however, these are protected under trademark law from use without permission on similar products or services);
- pseudonyms or professional or stage names (these may also be protected under trademark law or the law of unfair competition);
- mere variations on familiar symbols, emblems, or designs, such as typefaces, numerals, or punctuation symbols, and religious emblems or national symbols;
- information, research data, and bare historical facts (although many compilations of such information or data and extended expressions based on historical facts are protectable by copyright);
- blank forms, such as account ledger page forms, diaries,

address books, blank checks, restaurant checks, order forms, and the like (these record rather than convey information); and
- measuring and computing devices like slide rules or tape measures, calendars, height and weight charts, sporting event schedules, and other assemblages of commonly available information which contain no original material.

Utilitarian Aspects of Design

In addition, protection is specifically denied in the copyright statute to "utilitarian elements of industrial design." Pictorial, graphic, and sculptural works are, of course, protectable, but only insofar as their forms—the "mechanical or utilitarian aspects" of such designs—are not protected. The reasoning behind this provision is that if such aspects of otherwise decorative objects are to be protected at all, they must meet the rigorous requirements for a utility patent.

The question of what features of utilitarian objects copyright protects is most prevalent in the case of objects that have little ornamentation and consist mostly of a simple design that is largely determined by the function of the object. For instance, in the case of a ceramic lamp base decorated with painted ferns, the fern design has nothing to do with the function of the base—that of elevating the bulb and shade of the lamp to a height sufficient to illuminate the area surrounding the lamp—and is protectable by copyright.

However, a cylindrical brass lamp base fixed to a square marble foundation would embody no elements that were not primarily functional and would be unprotectable under the copyright statute. If a marble caryatid were substituted for the lamp's cylindrical brass base, the sculpture of the draped female figure would be protectable because of its more decorative and less utilitarian nature, even though it would still serve to elevate the lamp's bulb and shade. This principle of copyright law is easier to remember if you consider the general rule of copyright that the more elaborate and unusual the expression embodied in the work, the more protection the work is given (provided, of course, that the work is not copied from any other work).

Functional Works

Similarly, courts treat functional works like recipes, rules for games and contests, architectural plans, and computer programs somewhat differently from works that have no inherent functional aspects. Although they are eligible for copyright protection, protection for functional works is somewhat narrower than for other sorts of works. This is because the intended function of such a work dictates that certain standard information, symbols, and the like be included in the work and certain protocols be followed for the ordering and presentation of the information such works contain.

For example, copyright in recipes is very limited. Copyright does not protect any list of ingredients because such lists consist of information only and embody no protectable expression. A particular expression of recipe instructions *may* be protectable, at least from word-for-word copying, but probably only to the extent that the explanation of the steps in making the dish embodies expression that is not dictated by the necessary technique or inherent chemistry of the process. Courts have also held the view that very short explanations of concepts, such as game rules and recipes, are *not* copyrightable because granting copyright in them would effectively prevent any other recounting of such rules or recipes.

Copyright in Real Life

All this has a practical application. It may be that anyone is free to use the beautiful new typeface design that you worked nights and weekends to perfect, even though you intended it to be used only in a hand-lettered story you wrote for your niece's birthday. Or that great new slogan that you came up with to advertise your company's product may soon be on everyone's lips in contexts that don't help your sales for the quarter at all.

The good news is that if you design a poster calendar for your sporting goods company, you may copy from any other calendar all the information you need concerning the days of the week on which the dates fall and the dates of holidays and any information about the year's sporting events from schedules published in newspapers or by colleges, sports magazines, or anyone else. And when you compose the copy for ads for your business, you can make free use of slogans and catchphrases from popular culture without obtaining permission from the copyright owner of the work from which the slogan was taken; otherwise, you'd have to call up Edgar Rice Burroughs's heirs to use "Me Tarzan, you Jane," or George Lucas to use "May the Force be with you," in an ad.

However, a famous phrase or slogan of this sort may become so associated in the public's mind with its originator that it may not be used to sell products or services without the real threat of a suit for unfair competition. This means that the originator of a famous phrase or slogan could sue on the ground that your use of that phrase or slogan to market your product or service could cause consumers to associate your product or service with the originator of the phrase or slogan. Be very careful in employing a well-known phrase or slogan in any manner that displays it more prominently than, say, a line of text from a book or fragment of dialogue from a movie.

Copyright law treats facts of all sorts like ideas. The only thing relating to facts that is protectable under copyright law is the particular expression of those facts. You may write a movie script based on the historic facts surrounding the sinking of the *Titanic*; those facts are free for use by anyone who cares to gather them at the library or from other sources. However, if you believe that it's time for another movie about the *Titanic* and that Hollywood will buy your script, you may want to think twice before you mention your project to your cousin the screenwriter, since she is free to recognize your idea as a good one and write her own competing script based on the very facts you planned to use.

The same is true of plots. Shakespeare's *Romeo and Juliet* has spawned many works based on the plot of his play: the play *Abie's Irish Rose* and the movie *The Cohens and The Kellys*, now both forgotten except for the well-known copyright infringement suit concerning their similar plots, the famous musical *West Side Story*, the old television series *Bridget Loves Bernie*, and the 1969 Zeffirelli film *Romeo and Juliet*, which was only the latest in a long line of movies made from the Shakespeare play.

And if you think of the innumerable love songs written about heartbroken, jilted lovers, you will realize themes are not protectable by copyright either. Each of the 2,438,954 songs written about somebody's broken heart is a perfectly legitimate use of that theme. No doubt there will be more, similar, uses as long as popular music exists

Public Domain Material

The largest category of literary and artistic material which is not protected by copyright is "public domain" material. Most public domain material is material for which copyright protection has expired, such as the works of "dead poets"—literary gentlemen who have been dead a long time, like Shelley, Keats, and Shakespeare. The trick is to make sure that the author whose work you want to use has been dead long enough.

Herman Melville died in 1891. More important for purposes of determining the copyright status of his works is the fact that his books were written before 1891, which means that any rights Melville or his heirs had in them expired some time ago. This means that you may freely use Melville's *Moby Dick* characters and story in your screenplay. The same is not true of, for example, Tennessee Williams; even though he is just as dead as Melville, his plays are still protected. Williams's estate owns the copyrights in those plays and collects royalties from performances of them. All this applies to painters and composers too, as well as to lesser mortals like you and me whose creations are not quite great literature or art but are valuable to us nonetheless.

Figuring out whether a work is in the public domain is not simply a matter of determining whether the author has been dead a while, since the creators of many still-valid copyrights expired a long time before their copyrights will. Unless you know for sure that the copyright in a work has expired, you must investigate the copyright status of the work before reprinting it or adapting it or otherwise exercising any right reserved to the owners of valid copyrights.

At this writing, anything showing a copyright date more than seventy-five years ago is a safe bet. This may change if the duration of U.S. copyright protection is extended to expire seventy years after the death of an author (as opposed to the life-plus-fifty-years presently provided by the U.S. copyright statute). This change has been proposed in order to bring the United States into conformity with the longer term recently adopted by the countries of the European Union: The United Kingdom, The Irish Republic, France, Germany, Italy, Spain, Portugal, Greece, Denmark, The Netherlands, Belgium, and Luxembourg. (We will consider the duration of U.S. copyright protection at greater length in chapter 3.)

The best way to begin to determine whether a work is still protected by copyright is to consult the Checklist for the Preliminary Determination of the Copyright Status of a Work that ends chapter 3 and/or to follow the recommendations in the Copyright Office publication called "How to Investigate the Copyright Status of a Work," which is available free from the Copyright Office. (See chapter 4 for ordering information.)

You can also have the Copyright Office search its records for you. The fee for this service is $20 per hour. Call the Reference and Bibliography Section of the Copyright Office at (202) 707-6850 for their estimate of the time required for your search. You must fill out a formal search request form and send it with the estimated search fee before the Copyright Office will begin your search.

A faster way to conduct a copyright search is to hire a professional search firm to examine copyright records for you. Professional search firms charge larger fees for their services than the Copyright Office, but they probably will turn your search around much more quickly. The largest and perhaps the most reliable search firm is Thomson and Thomson. Call the Thomson and Thomson Copyright Research Group at (800) 356-8630 for a quotation of their fee for performing your search.

It is also possible to search Copyright Office files for registrations and related documents catalogued since January 1, 1978 via the Internet. You can connect to the Copyright Office Home Page on the World Wide Web at *http://lcweb.loc.gov/copyright*. There is no fee to connect to the Internet resources of the Copyright Office.

U.S. Government Works

There is one other category of public domain works of which you should be aware; that is works created by officers or employees of the U.S. government as a part of their government jobs. These works are in the public domain because the government has chosen not to claim copyright in works created at the taxpayers' expense.

This means that you may quote the entire text of a government publication on how to buy a car in your handbook for consumers without any special permission from the government. However, if your end creation consists predominantly of material produced by the government, your copyright notice should acknowledge the fact, as in: "Copyright 1996 Wilson St. Charles, except material reproduced on pages 21–40 and 64–89, which was taken from U.S. Government Publications 306A, 'New Car Buying Guide,' and 303A, 'Buying a Used Car.'"

The only precaution necessary before using material from government publications is to make sure that the material you want to use was prepared by the U.S. government proper and not by some private or semi-private agency of the government or a government contractor. You can probably do this by simply looking at the title page of the government publication or by calling the department or organization that published it. Anything published by the U.S. Government Printing Office or offered through the Consumer Information Catalog is almost certainly public domain material.

Copyright Notice

Copyright notice is an important tool in copyright protection. It is like a "No Trespassing" sign—notice to the world that you claim ownership of the copyright in the work to which it is affixed. The three elements of copyright notice should appear together in close proximity. The three elements of copyright notice are:

- the word "copyright" (that is C-O-P-Y-R-I-G-H-T, *not* "copywrite"), the abbreviation "Copr.," or the © symbol (or, in the case of a sound recording, the ℗ symbol). Even though it is often used by people who attempt to create the © symbol on a typewriter, the symbol (c) is not the equivalent of the © symbol. If you can't produce the © symbol, use the word "copyright" instead of the © symbol or draw the c-in-a-circle symbol by hand, but don't use parentheses in lieu of the circle—it's not the same. Because the word "copyright" and the abbreviation "Copr." are not recognized as a valid elements of copyright notice in some countries, it is preferable to use the © symbol if your work will or may be distributed outside the United States;

- the year of "first publication" of the work. For compilations or derivative works, the year of first publication of the compilation or derivative work should be used. "Publication" is defined as "the distribution of copies of a work to the public by sale or other transfer of ownership, or by rental, lease, or lending." However, the year-date of first publication may be omitted from copyright notice when a pictorial, graphic, or sculptural work, with any accompanying text, is reproduced on greeting cards, postcards, stationery, jewelry, dolls, toys, or other useful articles;

- the name of the owner of the copyright or an abbreviation or alternate name by which that copyright owner is generally recognized. For example, International Business Machines, Incorporated, can call itself "IBM" for purposes of copyright notice. However, when in doubt, use the form of your legal name you commonly use for other formal purposes, e.g., "Aaron L. Bowers" rather than "Sonny Bowers." If two or more people or other entities own the copyright, use all their names: "© 1998 Charles Dennis Wile and Christopher Lawrence Fort." Further, bear in mind that the *author* of the work may no longer be the *owner* of copyright in it.

In the United States, proper copyright notice consists only of some combination of the three elements mentioned above. All the following forms are correct: "Copyright 1997 Natalie Marie Wilson," "© 1997 N. M. Wilson," and ℗ 1997 Natalie M. Wilson" (for a sound recording). Countries that are signatories to the Buenos Aires Convention (see the discussion of copyright treaties below) require that "a statement of the reservation of the property right" in a work appear on or in the work for copyright protection. This means that for complete protection in Buenos Aires Convention countries, a statement asserting your ownership of your copyright and your reservation of the rights in it should be used in addition to the copyright notice described by the U.S. copyright statute that is also acceptable in Universal Copyright Convention countries. The most familiar form of such "reservation of rights" language is the phrase

"All rights reserved." This means that the form of copyright notice that guarantees the fullest protection available throughout the world is: "© 1997 William B. King, All rights reserved." You should use this form of notice, even if you do not anticipate that your work will be distributed outside the United States. Ink is cheap, but proper copyright notice can offer valuable benefits and protection.

Occasionally copyright owners will also add to the title page of a book or magazine something like this:

> No portion of this publication may be reproduced or transmitted in any form or by any means, electronic or mechanical, including by photo-copying, recording, or use of any information storage and retrieval system without express written permission from Pleasant View Press.

Besides scaring off some potential copyright infringers who may not know or appreciate the full significance of copyright notice, added language of this sort has no effect and is not a substitute for proper copyright notice. However, there is also nothing in copyright law that says you cannot use some language of this sort near your copyright notice to make more explicit your claim of ownership of copyright in your work.

The important thing to remember is that there is no legal subs-titute for proper copyright notice. It costs nothing to use and you don't need permission from anyone to use it. Not using notice on any work that leaves your hands is foolish.

When Notice Is Required

Foolish though it may be to fail to use copyright notice, it must be said that copyright notice is not *required* for any work published after March 1, 1989. That is the date the United States' entry into the Berne Convention became effective. The Berne Convention is a very old and widespread copyright treaty, but the United States became a signatory to it only in late 1988 for a variety of com-plicated reasons, one of which is that Berne Convention signatory countries may not require as a condition to copyright protection any "formalities," such as using copyright notice.

However, confusingly enough, the copyrights in works published before January 1, 1978, the effective date of the current copyright statute, may be *lost* in the United States if notice is not used.

Benefits of Using Notice

The short of this long story is that you cannot now lose copyright protection for any work published after March 1, 1989, by failing to use copyright notice. However, in order to encourage the use of copyright notice in the United States, the law provides a valuable procedural advantage in infringement lawsuits to copyright owners who do use it. Specifically, an infringer cannot successfully claim that he or she did not know that his or her act constituted copyright infringement if the copyright owner has used proper copyright notice. Being able to prove that a defendant willfully ignored such clear evidence that the plaintiff's work was protected by copyright has the effect of increasing the potential damages award available to a plaintiff, since courts are typically much harder on defendants who have intentionally violated plaintiffs rights.

That takes care of people dishonest enough to ignore copyright notice. Using copyright notice also precludes the possibility that honest people, seeing no copyright notice, will believe that your work is free for anyone to use. Even after Berne, copyright notice remains one of the most useful tools for protecting your copyright.

Placement of Copyright Notice

Copyright notice does not have to be obtrusive. Copyright Office regulations specify only that notice be placed, in a durable form affixed in a permanent manner, in a location on the work where it is reasonably easy to discover.

For works published in book form, acceptable locations for copyright notice include the title page, the page following the title page, either side of the front or back cover, and the first or last page of the main body of the book.

For motion pictures and other audiovisual works, notice should be embodied in the film or tape as a part of the image itself so that it will appear whenever the work is played or broadcast or otherwise performed and may be located with or near the title or credits or immediately following the beginning of the work or at or immediately preceding the end of the work.

If the audiovisual work lasts sixty seconds or less, copyright notice may appear in any of the locations specified above or on the leader of the film or tape immediately preceding the work if the notice is embodied there electronically or mechanically (that is, is not simply written by hand on the leader). For audiovisual works or motion pictures distributed to the public for private use, such as movie videotapes, notice may also appear on the permanent container for the work.

For pictorial, graphic, or sculptural works embodied in two dimensional copies, copyright notice should be affixed directly, durably, and permanently to the front or back of the copies or to the backing, mounting, or framing to which the copies are attached. For such works embodied in three-dimensional copies, notice should be affixed directly, durably, and permanently to any visible portion of the work or any base, mounting, framing, or other material to which the copies are attached. If, because of the nature of the work, it is impractical to affix notice to the copies directly or by means of a durable label, notice may appear on a tag or durable label which is designed to remain attached to the copy.

For copies of sound recordings, such as audiotapes, cassettes, and records, copyright notice should appear on the surface of the copy of the sound recording and on the container of the copy, so as to give reasonable notice to an observer of the claim of copyright ownership.

There are other sorts of works for which the Copyright Office prescribes placement of copyright notice. Further and more detailed information concerning copyright notice and placement is available in the free Copyright Office pamphlet "Copyright Notice," and in the Copyright Office circulars, also free, "Methods of Affixation and Positions of the Copyright Notice on Various Types of Works" and "Copyright Notice." Information on obtaining all three of these short publications is given at the end of chapter 4 of this book.

Geographic Limits of Protection

All rights of U.S. copyright owners are granted to them by the U.S. copyright statute, which is a federal law, that is, a law passed by Congress that governs copyright matters throughout the United States. The provisions of the federal copyright statute are interpreted by court decisions. These decisions become another segment of United States copyright law, for they are used by other courts in deciding later copyright cases.

It is important to realize that all this law skids to a halt at the geographic boundaries of the United States because, of course, U.S. laws have no jurisdiction outside the fifty states and possessions of the United States other than the more or less reciprocal recognition other countries grant U.S. copyrights under the various copyright treaties to which the United States is a party.

There are two situations in which geography and copyright combine to concern average creators or copyright owners. These are situations involving the protection of U.S. copyrights outside the United States and the circumstances under which the work of foreign nationals working in the United States are granted copyright protection by the U.S. copyright statute.

International Copyright Relations

Most other countries have their own copyright laws, the provisions of which may diverge considerably from those of our statute. For example, the term of copyright in Great Britain is different from that in the United States. Copyright treaties get around the fact that no country's law has any effect outside that country by documenting the agreements between countries that each will give the same recognition to the others' copyrights that it gives to its own citizens.

The United States is now a signatory to all the principal copyright treaties. These treaties are basically agreements among several nations that each treaty signatory will accord the same respect to the rights of copyright owners who are citizens of the other signatory countries that it does to those of its own citizens. In addition to the Berne Convention, which is the most important copyright treaty and offers the most protection to copyright owners, the United

States is a signatory to the Universal Copyright Convention and the Buenos Aires Convention. With the exception of China and the former U.S.S.R., most industrialized nations are signatories to one or more of the principal copyright treaties. To ensure protection for United States copyrights in countries that have not signed any of these copyright treaties or that ignore the rights of U.S. copyright owners, the United States has, where possible, entered bilateral treaties—that is, the treaties are signed only by the United States and the other nation.

Copyrighted works such as books, movies, television shows, and computer programs are important exports of the United States. However, in countries where the problems of poverty, disease, or war take precedence over the intellectual-property rights of citizens of other countries, and in nations such as China and the countries that once formed the U.S.S.R. which are still unfamiliar with the ideas of capitalism and private property, intellectual-property rights are given little or no respect. Protection against unauthorized use of copyrighted works in any particular country depends basically on the laws of that country; where the law is lax or non-existent or not enforced, U.S. companies suffer. For example, copyright piracy in China, which is reputed to have the highest incidence of copyright piracy in the world, costs U.S. companies approximately $827 million annually in recent years. Nearly $350 million of that amount has resulted from the 80 million pirated compact disks produced there yearly; nearly an equal amount is lost due to Chinese counterfeiting of U.S. computer software.

Perhaps these problems will be solved or ameliorated as a result of the United States' recent threats to restrict trade with China if China does not close down its dozens of factories producing counterfeit goods. The leaders of countries that make an industry of infringing U.S. copyrights are yielding to pressure from the United States to stop counterfeiters, who may have previously operated openly and without government interference. Increasingly, the U.S. government has enforced its citizens' copyright rights (as well as other intellectual-property rights, such as trademark and patent rights) by means of trade sanctions to punish nations that ignore U.S. intellectual-property rights. Like the 800 pound canary, the

United States wields considerable clout. Some of this clout comes from provisions affecting the recognition of intellectual property rights in trade agreements such as the recent North American Free Trade Agreement (NAFTA) and the General Agreement on Tariffs and Trade (GATT). Most of the United States' ability to coerce cooperation from other countries stems from the power of its collective pocketbook; many countries produce goods—or want to—for the U.S. market.

Such cooperation is necessary because no U.S. copyright owner can sue in the United States for copyright infringement that occurs elsewhere. If a U.S. CD is counterfeited in China and sold there or in another foreign country, the only recourse the U.S. copyright owner may have is to lobby the U.S. government to impose trade sanctions on China to compel it to shut down the infringer's operation. Similarly, some developing countries, even though they are signatories to one or more of the world's copyright treaties, do not impose meaningful penalties on infringers of foreign copyrights. This can make suing in one of these countries expensive and futile, because the only law that applies to infringements in other countries is the law of the country where the infringement occurs.

But if a foreign company brings its infringement to the U.S., the U.S. copyright owner can sue here. For example, a U.S. copyright owner cannot sue profitably in Somalia to stop the manufacture of infringing products because Somalia is not a signatory to any copyright treaty with the United States. However, if the infringing products are imported into the United States, the copyright owner can sue and can ask for seizure and destruction of the infringing products and any other remedy available under the U.S. copyright statute.

Foreign National Authors

A related question is that of the copyright status of works created by authors who are not U.S. citizens. Under certain conditions, the copyright statute limits the right of some foreign nationals to enjoy the protection of U.S. copyright law even if they create their otherwise copyrightable works within the United States.

The copyright statute says that published works of foreign nationals are protected if:

- on the date of first publication, one or more of the authors is a national or domiciliary of the United States, or of a foreign nation that is a party to a copyright treaty to which the United States is also a party, or is a stateless person, wherever that person may be domiciled; or
- the work is first published in the United States or in a foreign nation that, on the date of first publication, is a party to the Universal Copyright Convention; or
- the work is first published by the United Nations or any of its specialized agencies, or by the Organization of American States; or
- the work is a Berne Convention work; or
- the work comes within the scope of a presidential proclamation that extends protection to works of which one or more of the authors is, on the date of first publication, a national, domiciliary, or sovereign authority of a country that protects U.S. works on substantially the same basis as it protects works of its own citizens.

Any unpublished work is protected by U.S. copyright law, regardless of the citizenship of the author or in what country he or she resides.

U.S. citizens may register their copyrights in other countries, but such registration is not usually necessary. Protection for any U.S. work—to the same extent as is given to works of citizens of that country—is by operation of law granted to U.S. works by any country that is a signatory to one of the copyright treaties to which the United States is a party. Circular 38a, "International Copyright Relations of the United States," is available from the Copyright Office Forms Hotline (twenty-four hours a day, every day) at (202) 707-9100. This free publication contains general information about the treaties to which the United States is a signatory and specifies to what treaties each country of the world is a party. However, because copyright relations between the many countries of the world and the United States are in a constant state of flux and because new governmental regimes in some countries can create changed policies toward U.S. copyrights, if you are planning to market a valuable copyrighted work in a particular country or countries, it is a very good idea to consult a copyright lawyer before you publish the work.

Protecting Your Ideas

ECAUSE COPYRIGHT LAW does not protect ideas, methods, or systems, the best protection for valuable ideas (or methods or systems) is secrecy. Such ideas (etc.) are called "trade secrets" and are defined in the Uniform Trade Secrets Act (which is a reliable guide to trade secret law generally even though it has not been adopted by every state):

Information, including a formula, pattern, compilation, program, device, method, technique, or process, that: (i) derives independent economic value, actual or potential, from not being generally known to, and not being readily ascertainable by proper means by, other persons who can obtain economic value from its disclosure or use, and (ii) is the subject of efforts that are reasonable under the circumstances to maintain its secrecy.

There are, then, three requirements for trade secret protection:
- the secret must be maintained in secrecy;

- the secret must be novel (that is, not generally known in the pertinent trade or industry); and
- the secret must give its owner a competitive advantage over those who do not know or use it.

In addition, the owner of the trade secret must show the existence of a contractual or confidential relationship that prohibits the use or disclosure of the trade secret between the owner of the secret and the person or company that uses or discloses it.

Although copyright offers no protection for trade secrets, originators of such valuable ideas may create a legally enforceable contractual obligation by the careful use of a non-disclosure letter. (It's confusing, but these letters are also sometimes called "disclosure letters," as in, "I will *disclose* my trade secret to you but only on condition that you promise not to exploit it without me or tell anyone else about it.") Non-disclosure letters are merely agreements to preserve trade secrets that take the form of a letter. They may be used whenever the originator of an idea reveals the idea to someone who is in a position to exploit it. Examples of situations in which a non-disclosure letter would be useful to the originator of an idea, method, or system are:

- the submission of the prototype for a poster or calendar to a publisher;
- the submission of a business plan for using a 900 number in a novel way to a potential backer for the venture;
- the submission of a proposal for an improved system for managing the use of expensive medical equipment to a healthcare facility;
- the submission by an advertising agency of a proposed advertising campaign to a prospective client; or
- the submission of the prototype for a stuffed toy to a toy manufacturer.

Non-disclosure letters don't have to be long or contain particularly stern legal language in order to be effective. The form non-disclosure letter reproduced below will adequately protect you in most situations. Besides the legal effect of a non-disclosure letter, such a document also impresses upon the people to whom you submit your idea that you are claiming ownership of the idea and that you expect them to respect your rights in it. No written document can do much to impede the underhanded schemes of truly unethical people and the enforceability of the agreements contained in non-disclosure letters varies from state to state, so it is wise not to rely entirely on your non-disclosure letter to protect your idea. Although secrecy is still the best defense against the possibility that someone will exploit your idea without your participation, unless you own your own cannery, your method for preserving the vitamin content of canned vegetables will never earn you a penny unless you tell Hunt's or Del Monte about it. The most practical approach to protecting your trade secret is secrecy in combination with the judicious use of a non-disclosure letter.

Along these lines, there are several simple measures you can take to improve your chances of foiling anyone who may be inclined to appropriate your idea without your permission.

1. **Reduce it to writing.** Never simply describe your idea verbally to anyone to whom you submit it. Reduce your idea to a proposal, complete with a full written description of how your idea would work and could be exploited and drawings or photos of any prototype. (However, if it is possible to communicate your idea adequately without describing every facet of it, omit whatever you can from your proposal. This approach is the equivalent of removing the firing pin from a gun or neglecting to include the secret ingredient when you give your famous eggnog recipe to your neighbor. At the least, don't include in your proposal actual working diagrams drawn to scale—use a representational drawing that is unsuited for use in manufacture or delete important specifications from a working diagram before reducing it in size. The more complete the information included in your proposal, the more likely that someone could get the idea to eliminate you from the manufacturing loop.)

2. **Corral your proposal.** Put every element of the proposal that explains your idea into a presentation folder and number the copies of your proposal. This allows you to bring the right number of proposals to meetings with potential exploiters of your idea. It may not hurt to let the people to whom you give

copies of your proposal observe you writing the numbers of their copies opposite their names on a list of those who receive your proposal for review. Keep track of proposals that remain in the hands of others while they consider your idea and *get them back* so they don't float around in the file cabinets of some company looking for ideas or wind up in the hands of the unscrupulous brother-in-law or employee of someone who would never dream of using your idea without your permission.

3. ***Use copyright notice.*** Even though copyright notice is optional for works first published on or after March 1, 1989, and has never been required for unpublished works such as your proposal, using it on any copies of your proposal that leave your hands will indicate that you reserve your rights in that proposal. Copyright will not protect your basic idea, even if that idea is embodied in a written proposal, but it will protect your written and visual *expressions* of your idea. Copyright protection for your expressions of your idea offers no protection at all from the possibility that someone will read your proposal, comprehend your idea, and decide to execute it; use of a non-disclosure letter is designed to do this by documenting the promise of any person who signs it to refrain from exploiting your idea without permission. However, if someone who sees your proposal notes that you have included your copyright notice on it and believes that executing or exploiting your idea would somehow violate copyright law, that's not your problem. Copyright law is a matter of public record; if someone's misapprehensions about the law keep him or her from engaging in unethical behavior, so much the better. Use the following form of copyright notice for an unpublished work: "Unpublished work © Robert W. Wilson." (Do not use a year date, since this denotes the year of first publication of the work.) Use this legend on the title page of your proposal and on each separate element of it, such as a drawing or photograph.

4. ***Scare them.*** *In addition to* using copyright notice, you should include extra "no trespassing" language wherever your copyright notice appears. This extra language will have no actual legal effect but may have a certain *in terrorem* effect; that is,

it may scare people. Your scary language should be formal but shouldn't overstate the punishment an idea pirate will encounter. It should also include your name and address so that proposals that fall into the hands of anyone besides those you give them to can be returned. A good form for *in terrorem* language is: "All rights reserved. The design for a child's plush toy in the form of a black-and-white-polka-dot brontosaurus and the associated information embodied and disclosed in this document are strictly confidential proprietary information. Any disclosure of any feature of that design or any portion of that information may subject the person or entity making any such disclosure to legal action. To avoid liability, return this document promptly to Robert W. Wilson, 728 Williams Street, Murfreesboro, TN 37902."

5. **Warn them and be ready to walk.** Let everyone to whom you present your proposal know that you will be asking them to sign a copy of your non-disclosure letter *before* you present your idea to them. You may even consider sending the necessary copies of the non-disclosure letter in advance of your meeting in order that the people whom you expect to sign it may read and consider it. In any event, collect signed non-disclosure letters from everyone present when you meet with them to make your presentation. Make no exceptions; be prepared to call off the meeting if anyone refuses to sign.

6. **Don't sign their paper.** Never sign *their* non-disclosure letter. Not without the advice of a lawyer, anyway. Companies that often evaluate ideas that originate outside the organization sometimes offer people who have ideas to peddle form non-disclosure letters that are carefully drafted to give the companies the maximum latitude in using the ideas presented to them. It is unlikely that one of these non-disclosure letters will give you the protection you want; in fact, you may seriously diminish your bargaining power if you sign one. Many reputable companies will tell you up front that they will not look at your idea until you sign a non-disclosure letter. Ask for a copy of their form letter and take it to a lawyer for an explanation and possible negotiation of terms more favorable to you before signing it.

FORM NON-DISCLOSURE LETTER

for use in submitting ideas, methods, or systems to those who could exploit them for profit

Robert W. Wilson[1]
728 Williams Street
Murfreesboro, TN 37902
November 20, 1996[2]

Jarvis Bigshot, Vice President[3]
The Cuddly Toy Company[4]
21784 Industrial Drive
Madison, Wisconsin 20087

Dear Mr. Bigshot,[5]

I am today submitting to you for your consideration my idea and design[6] for[7] a child's plush toy in the form of a black-and-white polka-dot brontosaurus named "Bronte" containing a microchip device that plays the melody for the song "Dem Bones" when the stomach area of the toy is depressed.

I submit my prototype design and the documents that express, explain, and illustrate it to you at your request and with the purpose of allowing you to consider entering a formal, written agreement with me whereby I would grant The Cuddly Toy Company[8] the right to develop, manufacture, and market products based on my design.

My disclosure to you of the information embodied in my prototype and in the documents submitted with it is made in confidence and in consideration of your promise that neither you individually nor your company will disclose or reveal any part or portion of the ideas or design embodied in that prototype or those documents, that you individually and in your capacity as an officer, employee, or agent of The Cuddly Toy Company[9] will exercise your best efforts to diligently guard against any disclosure to any other person or entity of any of the information or ideas embodied in the submitted materials or of the existence of my design or its description or the concept upon which it is based.

You further promise that no use or exploitation of any sort whatsoever of my design or of any portion of the information embodied in the documents I submit to you, whether protected under patent or copyright laws or not, will be made by you or The Cuddly Toy Company[10] until and unless a written document setting out fully the terms of any agreement that may be reached between me and The Cuddly Toy Company[11] is executed by me and an authorized representative of your company. You agree that any use by you or The Cuddly Toy Company[12] of any of the information, ideas, concepts, inventions, or other features embodied in the materials I submit to you today would cause me irreparable harm and entitle me to money damages and an injunction preventing your further such actions.

You further agree to return promptly to me all the materials I submit to you today upon my request or on or before a date ten business days[13] after our meeting, whichever occurs first.

If you agree to the foregoing terms, please countersign this letter in the space provided below and return it to me.

Sincerely,

Robert Wilson[14]

Agreed and accepted:

The Cuddly Toy Company[15]

By: _____ ,[16] an authorized signatory
SIGNATURE

_____ 17
PRINT NAME HERE

FORM NON-DISCLOSURE LETTER: NOTES

1. Insert your name and address here, or use stationery preprinted with your name and address.

2. Use the date of your meeting with the person or company to whom you are submitting your idea.

3. Insert the name and title of each person with whom you arrange to meet. Take pains to use the correct name and title. Your aim is to document the names of the people who see your proposal and, if you are submitting your idea to a company, to reflect in the non-disclosure letter that those people are acting in their official capacity as agents for the company that employs them (i.e., that the actions of the individuals to whom you disclose your idea are attributable to their employer).

4. In addition to preparing a copy of your non-disclosure letter for each person whom you know will attend the meeting at which you present your idea, prepare several copies of the letter with only the name and address of the organization in the inside address location on the letter. This will allow you to pass out these generic copies of your letter to unexpected attendees who show up at your presentation meeting.

5. Insert the name of the person to whom the letter is addressed.

6. For a method, use "method"; for a system, use "system" instead of "idea and design." Adjust other language in this form letter according to your use of it, bearing in mind that specific, unambiguous language is essential if an agreement is to be easily interpreted by the parties or, potentially, the judge in a later lawsuit.

7. In this space insert a description of the idea, method, or system you hope to protect by using a non-disclosure letter. The goal here is to describe your idea with enough specificity that anyone who later examines the non-disclosure letter can determine just what it was that the person who countersigns it agreed not to disclose.

8. Insert the name of the company to which you are submitting your idea, method, or system.

9. Insert the name of the company to which you are submitting your idea, method, or system.

10, 11, 12. Insert the name of the company to which you are submitting your idea, method, or system.

13. Use common sense in determining how long to leave copies of your proposal with the company that sees it. No business executive is going to make a decision on the spot to develop and market your design; on the other hand, giving a company a set period of time within which to decide whether it wants to exploit your idea is smart. Ask the person with whom you arrange your presentation meeting how long it will take for his or her staff to evaluate your proposal and use that time period, if it is reasonable, as the consideration period you specify in your non-disclosure letter.

14. Type your name here, leaving space for your signature above your typed name.

15. Insert the name of the company to which you are submitting your idea, method, or system.

16. Leave this space blank for the signature of the person who countersigns the letter.

17. Leave this space blank for the printed name of the person who countersigns the letter.

Even with careful and consistent use of a non-disclosure letter, trade secret protection will be lost if:
- the owner of the trade secret fails to keep it secret;
- a third party independently discovers the secret; or
- a third party who is not under a contractual obligation to preserve the trade secret discovers the trade secret by careful analysis of the product that embodies the secret.

One of the most common defenses raised by defendants in trade secret misappropriation suits is that the trade secret is no longer a secret. However, the requirement that the owner of a trade secret keep it secret is not absolute. The owner must merely take "reasonable measures" to preserve his or her secret. Some of the measures that courts have considered in determining the sufficiency of the efforts of trade secret owners to maintain secrecy are:
- the requirement by the trade secret owner that employees of the owner sign a non-disclosure agreement;
- the requirement by the trade secret owner that employees of the owner sign a non-competition agreement;
- the degree of physical security of the trade secret owner's facilities, such as office space, equipment, and computer systems, including whether the owner maintains records, etc., that explain the trade secret in a secure location and whether a log book is kept to record the location of each copy of such confidential information;
- the trade secret owner's policy to reveal the trade secret only on a "need-to-know" basis;

- the efforts of the trade secret owner to educate employees of the owner as to what is secret and the proper uses of such secret information;
- the use by the trade secret owner of proprietary legends on products that embody the trade secret;
- the efforts of the trade secret owner to diminish the likelihood of disclosure of the trade secret by debriefing departing employees of the owner and reminding those employees of their continuing obligation to preserve the trade secret; and
- the requirement by the trade secret owner that departing employees of the owner sign a termination agreement that acknowledges the employee's understanding of his or her continuing obligation to preserve the trade secret.

Because trade secret owners (at least those who turn up in reported court decisions) are more often companies than individuals, these factors may seem to have little applicability to an individual who has a valuable secret to protect. However, even a trade secret owner who operates his or her business out of a spare bedroom and has no regular employees may encounter situations in which an awareness of the importance of efforts to preserve secret information is necessary. For instance, a trade secret owner may hire a typist to help reduce to an organized, written form the documents that explain the secret; the typist should be asked to sign a non-disclosure letter, should be required to do the typing on the premises of the owner rather than taking confidential materials to another workplace, and should be warned not to talk about any of the information embodied in the material to be typed.

It also must be noted that although affixing a copyright notice to materials that contain a trade secret does not result in loss of trade secret protection, copyright registration may do so if care is not used in the preparation of the deposit material that must accompany any registration application. Because the information contained in a copyright registration, including the content of the work being registered, is public record, trade secret owners must take measures to avoid disclosing confidential information. For example it is possible to deposit only a portion of the work when registering certain machine-readable works, such as computer programs, omitting from the deposited portion any trade secret information. It is also possible to request from the Copyright Office special relief from registration deposit requirements so that an "identifying portion" of the work can be deposited rather than the entire work. Call a Copyright Information Specialist (202) 707-9100 at the Copyright Office to discuss whether there is a way to register the copyright in material that embodies your trade secret without making your secret public. (See chapter 4 for more on copyright registration and the deposits required for registration.)

CHAPTER 3

Copyright Duration

C REATIVE PEOPLE OFTEN believe that copyright law is a dark mystery, accessible only to lawyers, and that the mechanisms of copyright protection are incredibly complex. Fortunately, they're wrong.

"Copyright protection" means the protection the law gives copyright owners from unauthorized use of their works. As a general rule, the U.S. copyright statute protects all varieties of literary, musical, dramatic, choreographic, pictorial, graphic, sculptural, and audiovisual works and sound recordings as soon as they are fixed in what the statute calls any "tangible medium of expression." Copyright protection lasts a very long time. Copyrights in works created today will not expire until well into the next century and many copyrights in works dating from the early decades of this century are still valid. The period of time during which the law offers copyright protection to a particular work is called the "term of copyright."

Determining Copyright Duration

There are two primary reasons why you may want to determine the copyright status of a work. They are: (1) that you want to determine whether the copyright in the work has expired, thereby transforming the work into a public domain work, which means that you may use the work in any way without permission from anyone; and (2) that you want to contact the owner of copyright in a work which is still protected to ask permission to use the work.

Determining the term of copyright for a work is not hard if you know a few things about when, by whom, and under what circumstances the work was created. The initial question to ask in determining the copyright status of any work is whether the work was created before or after January 1, 1978. Copyright protection for any work created *before* that date, which is the date the current United States copyright statute went into effect, is governed by the provisions of the previous copyright statute, the Copyright Act of 1909. Protection for any work created on or after January 1, 1978 is governed by the present copyright statute, the Copyright Act of 1976. (The present statute was voted into law in 1976; it became effective January 1, 1978.)

Copyright protection for any eligible work created on or after January 1, 1978 commences at the moment the work is first "fixed" in any tangible form. This protection is automatic: no action by the author of the work is necessary to begin it; the mere act of creating a work that qualifies for copyright protection triggers that protection. How long copyright protection endures for any such work largely depends upon its author or authors. For purposes of determining the duration of copyright, the copyright statute divides works into basic categories and specifies a term for each category of work. These categories of works and their corresponding terms are discussed below.

Works Created by Individual Authors

Copyright in a work created by an individual author vests in that author from the inception of the work. The copyright in a work created by an individual author will endure until fifty years after his or her death. This rule for determining the duration of copyright protection for a work by an individual author applies even if the author assigns or licenses the copyright in the work to someone else.

The Copyright Office maintains records concerning the deaths of authors of copyrighted works. In addition, in order to make the determination of the expiration dates of copyrights easier, the copyright statute provides that "any person having an interest in a copyright" may notify the Copyright Office that the author of the work embodying that copyright has died or is still living. Information is also gathered from Copyright Office records and from other sources.

Anyone seeking information about an old copyright in a work by an obscure author may be able to obtain a certified report from the Copyright Office that states that there is nothing in the records of the Copyright Office to indicate that the author is living or died within the previous fifty years. Anyone who uses a work that, in reliance on such a report, he or she in good faith believes to have fallen into the public domain may use the report as a defense if the author of the work, or the author's heirs, bring suit for copyright infringement on the ground that the copyright in the work is still valid.

Under the present statute, all copyright terms expire at the end of the calendar year. This means if you write a short story in 1998, copyright protection begins as soon as you have written your story, whether it is handwritten, typed on a typewriter, entered into a computer, or even recorded onto an audiocassette. Copyright protection for your story will expire at the end of the fiftieth year after your death; if you die in January of 2051, your story will be protected by copyright through December 31, 2101.

Joint Works

The copyright statute says that if two or more people create a work "with the intention that their contributions be merged into inseparable or interdependent parts of a unitary whole," those people are "joint authors" and the work they create is a "joint work." To qualify as one of the joint authors of a work, a person must contribute copyrightable expression to the work; someone who contributes only an unembellished idea to a work is not a joint author of the work.

Joint authors of a work share equally in any profits created by an exploitation of the work unless the authors agree otherwise at the time of the creation of the work. With the limitation that he or she may not grant an exclusive license to use a work without permission from the other author or authors of the work, a joint author may exploit the work without the permission of any other joint author. However, the exploiting author must share the profits derived from any such exploitation with the other joint author or authors. The copyright in a joint work endures until fifty years after the death of the last surviving author.

Anonymous and Pseudonymous Works

The copyright statute says that an anonymous work is a "work on the copies or phonorecords of which no natural person is identified as author." A pseudonymous work is defined as a "work on the copies or phonorecords of which the author is identified under a fictitious name." Even if the identity, or in the case of pseudonymous works, the real identity, of the author of an anonymous or pseudonymous work is known, unless the real name of the author appears on the copies or phonorecords of the work, the work will be treated as an anonymous or pseudonymous work. The status of a work as an anonymous or pseudonymous work has an important effect on the duration of copyright protection for the work.

The term of copyright for an anonymous or pseudonymous work is seventy-five years from the year of first publication of the work, or one hundred years from the year of its creation, whichever expires first. However, the copyright statute also provides that any person having an interest in the copyright in an anonymous or pseudonymous work may convert the term of copyright protection for the work to a term measured by the life or lives of the author or authors of the work plus fifty years. This is accomplished by simply filing with the Copyright Office, at any time before seventy-five years after the work's publication or one hundred years after its creation, a statement that identifies the authors or one of the authors of the work. This has the effect of converting the term of copyright for the work to the life-plus-fifty-years measurement that applies to individual works.

The new copyright statute has not been in effect long enough to allow the heirs or assigns of any anonymous or pseudonymous author who disclosed his or her real name to the Copyright Office during his or her lifetime to determine if, by that action, the term of copyright in the formerly anonymous or pseudonymous work was enlarged. However, depending upon the age at which an author creates an anonymous or pseudonymous work and how many years the author lives thereafter, disclosing the author's name to the Copyright Office may, indeed, have the effect of prolonging copyright protection for the work. Therefore, this provision of the copyright statute is something that any anonymous or pseudonymous author and anyone who acquires the copyright in an anonymous or pseudonymous work should keep in mind.

Although most authors are proud to affix their names to their works, there are some circumstances when the anonymity of an author is desirable. Perhaps the most common example of this is the ghostwritten celebrity "autobiography." Anyone who thinks about it may readily realize that the movie star or rock star or statesman whose "autobiography" is the newest addition to the bestseller list did not personally spend six months of eight-hour days in front of a computer, and that the hard work of researching and writing the book was performed by someone else. However, it is often the case that the celebrity's name is the only name that appears on the book's dust jacket or copyright page. The ghostwriter for the book may be mostly responsible for the book's appeal and cohesiveness, and may be contractually entitled to a fat fee for writing the book and/or a generous share of the royalties produced by its sale, but, in the same contract that entitles him or her to be paid, the ghostwriter may have agreed to keep his or her role in creating the book a secret.

Works Made for Hire

Works made for hire are the only category of work in which the copyright does not initially vest in the creators of those works. The most common variety of works made for hire are works prepared by employees within the scope of their employment. The present copyright statute also specifies nine categories of specially commissioned works created by independent contractors as appropriate for works made for hire, provided that the party who commissions the work and the freelancer who creates it agree in writing that the work is to be considered a work made for hire. (See chapter 7 for a more detailed discussion of works made for hire.)

The term of copyright for a work made for hire is seventy-five years from the year of first publication of the work, or one hundred years from the year of its creation, whichever expires first.

Pre-1978 Works

Determining whether a work created before January 1, 1978 (while the 1909 copyright statute was still in effect) is protected by copyright may be a complicated undertaking.

Under the previous copyright statute, a work was entitled to an initial twenty-eight-year term of copyright protection. This initial term was measured from the date the work was first published with copyright notice. At the end of the first twenty-eight-year term of protection, copyright could be renewed for an additional twenty-eight years, for a total of fifty-six years of copyright protection. If renewal was not made, the copyright in the work was lost and the work fell into the public domain. This sometimes lead to the unfortunate result that some authors earned nothing in old age from their years of creative labor because the copyrights in their works had expired.

In drafting the present copyright statute, our legislators tried to remedy this situation by eliminating the renewal concept for works created on or after January 1, 1978. In addition, they extended copyright protection for works created under the previous copyright statute that were still protected by copyright under that statute when the new statute went into effect. Copyright protection for works that were in their renewal terms on January 1, 1978 was extended by nineteen years; this meant that the term of protection for those works was enlarged to a total of seventy-five years. Works that were in their initial twenty-eight-year term of protection on January 1,

1978 still had to be renewed at the end of that term; they, too, were granted extended renewal terms of forty-seven years for a total of seventy-five years of protection.

In spite of this bonanza for the owners of pre-1978 copyrights, many of these older copyrights continued to be lost because of the failure to renew them. A very large percentage of pre-1978 works therefore entered the public domain after only twenty-eight years of copyright protection.

To even things up a bit between the owners of pre-1978 copyrights and copyrights created under the present statute, the law was changed in 1992. The new law, the Copyright Renewal Act of 1992, made renewal automatic for pre-1978 works first published between January 1, 1964 and December 31, 1977. Owners of pre-1978 copyrights may still file renewal forms and, in fact, are encouraged to do so, but no such action is *required* to secure the forty-seven additional years of protection granted to these older works. Certain benefits, such as the presumption that the statements made in the renewal certificate are valid, accrue to those who do file timely renewal certificates.

If no renewal was made for works published *before* 1964, those works have fallen into the public domain, which is an irrevocable state of copyright outer-darkness that no one can alter.

Unpublished Works

Unpublished works created before January 1, 1978 fall into a special class of works as regards the term of copyright protection.

The current copyright statute provides that works created prior to 1978 that have neither been published or registered for copyright will be protected in the same way that post-1977 works are protected. That is, the term of copyright protection for such a work created by an individual is the life of the author plus fifty years (or the life of the last surviving author plus fifty years, for joint works). If the work is anonymous, pseudonymous, or a work made for hire, the term of protection is seventy-five years from the year of first publication of the work, or one hundred years from the year of its creation, whichever expires first.

The present copyright statute provides that works created prior to 1978 but published only *after* January 1, 1978 cannot expire before December 31, 2002. Further, if such a pre-1978 work is published between January 1, 1978 and December 21, 2003, its copyright cannot expire before December 31, 2027. These periods of protection are not affected by the date of the death of the authors of such works.

This provision has interesting implications for anyone who has an ancestor who kept a diary or was a novelist or composer. Old manuscripts and other works that would have become public domain many years ago had they been published prior to 1978 may be eligible for copyright protection well into the next century.

CHECKLIST FOR *PRELIMINARY* DETERMINATION OF THE COPYRIGHT STATUS OF A WORK

Unpublished Works

- Examine your copy of the work in question.
- If there is any indication that the work has not been published (if, for instance, you know of its existence only in manuscript form), examine it closely for a copyright notice or other indication of publication. Unless and until you find clear evidence (for example, such as locating a printed copy in a library of a novel you possess in manuscript form) that the work has been published,* assume that it is an unpublished work.
- The term of protection for works created prior to 1978 that have not been published or registered for copyright is the life of the author plus fifty years in the case of individual authors;* the life of the last surviving author plus fifty years, for joint works;* and seventy-five years from the year of first publication of the work,* or one hundred years from the year of its creation,* whichever expires first, in the case of anonymous or pseudonymous works and works made for hire.*
- The term of protection for works created prior to 1978 that were published only *after* January 1, 1978* cannot expire before December 31, 2002. Further, if such a pre-1978 work is published between January 1, 1978 and December 21, 2003,* the copyright in it cannot expire before December 31, 2027. These periods of protection are not affected by the date of the death of the authors of such works.

Works First Published Prior to 1978

- Look at the copyright notice for the work in question. If there is no copyright notice on a work published prior to 1978, it is likely that the copyright in the work has been lost.*
- If the year of first publication in the copyright notice is prior to 1978, the work was first published under the 1909 Copyright Act.
- If the year date in the copyright notice is 1963 or earlier, the initial term of copyright protection expired twenty-eight years after the year given in the copyright notice, *if* no renewal of copyright was made.* If copyright renewal was made, copyright protection for the work will expire or has expired seventy-five years after the year of first publication given in the copyright notice.
- If the year date in the copyright notice is 1964 or later, the copyright in the work was or will be renewed automatically twenty-eight years after the year of first publication given in the copyright notice and will not expire until seventy-five years after that year.

Works First Published after 1977

- Look at the copyright notice for the work in question. If there is no copyright notice on a work published between January 1, 1978 and March 1, 1989, copyright in the work *may* have been lost if, within five years after the work was first published without notice, the work was not registered with the Copyright Office and no effort was made to add copyright notice to copies of the work that were distributed after the omission was discovered.*
- If the year of first publication in the copyright notice is after 1977, the work was first published under the 1976 Copyright Act.
- If the name of only one individual is reflected as the author of the work,* the copyright in the work will expire fifty years after the death of that author.
- If there are two or more names reflected as the authors of the work,* the copyright in the work will expire fifty years after the death of the last surviving author.
- If the name reflected on copies of the work as the author of the work is a pseudonym,* the work is a "pseudonymous work" and the term of copyright for the work is seventy-five years from the year of first publication of the work, or one hundred years from the year of its creation, whichever expires first.*

- If no author name is given on copies of the work or the author is merely referred to as "Anonymous," the work is an "anonymous work,"* and the term of copyright for the work is seventy-five years from the year of first publication of the work, or one hundred years from the year of its creation, whichever expires first.*
- If no individual's name is reflected on copies of the work as the author of the work or some notation such as "Compiled by the editors of Magellan Press, Inc." appears as the credit line on copies of the work, the work may be a work made for hire.* (This conclusion cannot be made merely from the fact that the copyright notice for the work includes the name of a company rather than an individual, since authors sometimes assign their copyrights to publishers, an action that does not affect the duration of copyright.) The term of copyright for a work made for hire is seventy-five years from the year of first publication of the work, or one hundred years from the year of its creation, whichever expires first.

CHECKLIST: NOTES

* None of the conclusions marked with an asterisk can be safely made without examination of Copyright Office records regarding the work in question or other reliable information about the circumstances surrounding the creation of the work obtained from other sources. This checklist is intended only to demonstrate the observations that must be made in determining the copyright status of a work and is not sufficient and *is not intended to be sufficient* to produce a firm conclusion of copyright status in many situations. For example, because copyright notice is no longer required to appear on published works, some copyright owners may omit it. However, since copyright protection does not depend on the use of copyright notice, the absence of notice on a work is not necessarily an indication that the copyright in the work is no longer valid. As you work your way through the checklist, consider your encounter with an asterisk a signal that you cannot determine the copyright status of the work in question without obtaining further information that is not available to you by mere examination of the work. A checklist paragraph that bristles with asterisks is the equivalent of the warning "do not attempt this at home."

Using the Works of Others

Once you have definitely determined the copyright status of a work, there are two avenues open to you.

If you are certain that the copyright in the work has expired, you may safely use the work in any way, including exercising any of the rights reserved to owners of valid copyrights. This means that you can adapt Charlotte Bronte's novel, *Jane Eyre,* for a screenplay; set Ben Jonson's poem, "Though I am young and cannot tell," to music; reprint all or any portion of Ralph Waldo Emerson's essay on self-reliance; adapt and record Johann Pachelbel's Canon for use as a film soundtrack; print and sell reproductions of Leonardo da Vinci's famous painting, Mona Lisa; create a poster from a photograph by the very early photographer Julia Margaret Cameron; or create and sell copies of Michelangelo's sculpture, *David.*

If you find that the copyright in the work you want to use is still valid, you must request from the owner of copyright in that work permission to use the work in the manner you have planned. Finding the owner of copyright in a work (as opposed to the *author* of the work, who may not own the copyright in the work anymore) may be easy or difficult, depending on the circumstances.

With a poem or play or book or any other published literary work, write the "Permissions Department" of the publisher of the work to request permission to use it. If the publisher is not the owner of copyright in the work, it will certainly have been licensed to publish it and, depending upon the nature of the use for which you request permission, will grant or deny your request or forward your letter to the author of the work for his or her consideration.

Copyrights in popular songs and other contemporary musical compositions are usually owned by music publishers. If you call one of the performing rights societies that collects royalties for broadcast uses of musical compositions, BMI (212) 586-2000 or ASCAP (212) 621-6000 or SESAC (212) 586-3450, with the title of the composition and the name of the songwriter or composer, you can determine the name of the publisher of the composition, from whom you should request permission to use it.

For works of the visual arts, such as paintings or sculptures, you should contact the artist directly or, in the case of a deceased artist, the artist's estate. Galleries and museums may be good sources for such address information. However, do not assume that because a painting is owned by a museum or an individual collector that the copyright in the painting or sculpture is also owned by the museum or collector. Although the owner of a painting or sculpture is, of course, allowed to display it, ownership of a work of art does not automatically bestow on the owner of the work the right to exercise any of the other exclusive rights of copyright. As with any other sort of copyrighted work, your request to reproduce or otherwise use the work should be addressed to the owner of copyright in the work, even if it takes some detective work to figure out just who this is.

Permissions

Unless you are certain that your intended use of a copyrighted work will qualify as a "fair use" of that work, you should secure consent to use the work from the owner of the copyright in the work *before* you use it. Such consents, which are actually licenses of copyright (discussed in chapter 7), are usually called "permissions."

Permissions do not have to take any particular form. In fact, *non-exclusive* licenses, which is what most permissions are, don't even have to be in writing to be effective. However, it is a bad idea to depend on anyone's ability to recall the terms of a verbal license.

This means that you should request any permission in writing. Fortunately, permissions are simple enough documents that you will probably be able yourself to secure any permissions you need. The simplest form for requesting a permission is a letter that includes a space for the counter-signature of the person who is in a position to grant your request to use a copyrighted work. If all the terms of the proposed permission are stated unambiguously in the body of the letter, the signature at the bottom of the letter of the person to whom the letter is addressed, indicating his or her consent to those terms, will transform the letter into a binding agreement. Chapter 7 discusses written agreements in more depth and the Appendix of this book includes a simple permission letter that may be used as a model for any letter of this sort.

Nothing compels anyone to whom you write for permission to use a work to grant your request. Some materials such as unpublished letters and manuscripts may contain confidential or embarrassing information or comments, at least in the view of the person who wrote them or whose famous relative wrote them. This means that permission request letters should be polite and deferential. Further, although many permission requests are granted without payment, it may be that offering even a small amount in return for the requested permission will decrease your chances of being turned down. After all, if the material you want to use is important to your project, it is probably valuable enough to pay for.

One word of warning about requesting permissions. Never decide to use a copyrighted work after you have been denied permission to do so. Your transgression will be no greater than it would have been if you had never requested such permission, but your action in defiance of the denial of permission to use the work is likely to anger the owner of the copyright in the work. Anger is an important ingredient in lawsuits. Further, your earlier request for permission to use the work may be used against you in court as evidence that the claimed infringement was not an innocent blunder.

A far better course if you are denied permission to use a work that is critical to your own project is to write again to the person from whom you must secure permission to use the work. In this second letter, if you think that doing so would help your case, recount your credentials as a scholar, journalist, artist, critic, or the like. Describe your project in detail and emphasize the value of the copyright you want to use to the project as a whole. Finally, acknowledge the reservations of the copyright owner, but politely ask him or her to reconsider your request to use the copyrighted work. You may even ask your publisher, if you have one, or a scholar who is noted in your field to write a similar letter. This sort of second assault may not produce the permission you want, but it can't hurt; the worst that can happen is that the copyright owner will say no again or will not reply to your letter. All that means is that you are still where you were. However, as mentioned above, it also means that you should restructure your project, substituting another work for the one you wanted to use, or, if your project is really dependent on the work you have been denied permission to use, abandon it. An unfinished project, no matter how brilliantly conceived, is preferable to a lawsuit for copyright infringement any day.

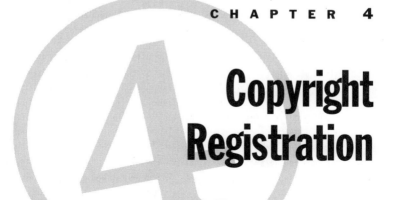

CHAPTER 4

Copyright Registration

Y OU PROBABLY DON'T need a lawyer to help you properly
register your copyright, but you do need to educate
yourself about registration in order to avoid mistakes.

The Copyright Office

The Copyright Office in Washington, D.C. is the federal agency that
has the responsibility for administering the registration of copyrights
and performing other government functions relating to copyrights,
such as maintaining records of copyright registrations and creating
and disseminating regulations interpreting sections of the copyright
statute. The Copyright Office is a division of the Library of Congress;
copies of works registered for copyright may end up in the collections of the Library, depending on the work and the needs and
collections policies of the Library.

There is no such thing as any state copyright law. That means that
there is no state agency anywhere in the United States that grants

copyright registrations or otherwise has anything to do with copyrights. All U.S. copyright registrations are granted by the Copyright Office; whether it is a child's poem or a hit song or the screenplay for a blockbuster movie, if it is registered for copyright in the United States, it is registered in the Copyright Office in Washington.

"Poor Man's Copyright"

A short digression concerning a persistent piece of folklore called "poor man's copyright" is in order. "Poor man's copyright" is a homemade and virtually worthless would-be substitute for copyright registration. It supposedly works like this: you finish your novel (or song or computer program), seal the manuscript (or cassette recording or computer diskette) in an envelope, and mail it to yourself. You then preserve the postmarked envelope, unopened, against the day that you dramatically rip it open in court, where you use the dated, sealed envelope to demonstrate that your work existed in a certain form on a certain date, thereby proving either that any similarities between your work and the work of the person who has sued you for infringement are coincidental, since your work existed before the plaintiff's work, *or* that the similarities between your work and the work of the person you have sued for infringe-ment are *not* coincidental, since your work existed before the defendant's work. It doesn't really work this way in real life. In real life, there is no legal substitute for copyright registration, which is the only event that courts recognize as sufficient to accomplish what copyright registration accomplishes.

Other similar repositories for unpublished creative works, such as that operated by the Writers Guild of America (a screenwriters' union) and other organizations for creative people working in a particular medium, are no more worthwhile as a *substitute* for copyright registration, whatever else they may accomplish. (For example, to protect themselves from accusations that they have stolen material from scripts that they have not bought, many studios and producers will not read a script *unless* it is registered with the Writers Guild.) Spend your money and time to register your copyright with the Copyright Office. It won't hurt to mail a copy of your work to yourself or place it in some registry *in addition* to registering your copyright, but nothing can substitute legally for copyright registration. Depositing a copy of your work with a reliable registry can be a pretty good cheap substitute for the full-term retention of a copy of your work by the Copyright Office (discussed below), even though it is likely that, periodically, you will need to renew your deposit contract with any such registry.

Copyright Registration Forms

The Copyright Office prescribes a specific form for the registration of copyright in each particular variety of work. It is important to use the right type of copyright registration form to register your work. The types of registration forms and the sorts of works they register are:

- *Form TX* is used for non-dramatic literary works, including all types of published and unpublished works written in words or other verbal or numerical symbols, except for dramatic works and certain kinds of audiovisual works. You will need this form to register a work that is a fiction or non-fiction book, story, or article, a poem or collection of poems, a directory, a catalog, a print advertisement, a computer program, a data base, or another sort of non-dramatic literary work.
- *Form PA* is used for works of the performing arts, including published and unpublished works prepared for the purpose of being performed directly before an audience or indirectly by means of any device or process. Some examples of works in this category are: musical works (including any accompanying words); dramatic works (including any accompanying music); pantomimes and choreographic works; and motion pictures and other audiovisual works.
- *Form VA* is used for published and unpublished pictorial, graphic, and sculptural works, including two-dimensional and three-dimensional works of fine, graphic, and applied art, photographs, prints, and art reproductions, maps, globes, charts, technical drawings, diagrams, models, pictorial or graphic labels and advertisements, as well as "works of artistic craftsmanship." Use Form VA if the work consists mainly

of pictorial and graphic material; use Form TX if it consists mainly of text.

- *Form SR* is used for sound recordings, that is, works that result from the fixation of a series of musical, spoken, or other sounds. Form SR should be used to register the claim to copyright in the sound recording itself. Form SR may also be used to register both the sound recording and the musical, dramatic, or literary work fixed in the phonograph record (or tape, CD, or cassette) as long as the same person or organization owns the copyright in both the sound recording and in the work that was recorded.

- *Form SE* is used for serials, that is, all works issued or intended to be issued in successive parts bearing numerical or chronological designations and intended to be continued indefinitely, such as periodicals, newspapers, magazines, newsletters, annuals, journals, etc.

- *Form RE* is used for any application to renew the copyright in a work, regardless of the sort of work. A renewal application can be made only for works that were already in their first twenty-eight-year term of copyright protection on January 1, 1978 (namely, works originally copyrighted between January 1, 1950 and December 31, 1977). Renewals can be made only during the last calendar year of the first twenty-eight-year copyright term. Since 1992, renewal of copyrights for works first published between January 1, 1964 and December 31, 1977 has been automatic. Owners of such copyrights may still file renewal forms, but no such action is required to secure the forty-seven additional years of protection granted to these older works by the present copyright statute.

- *Form CA* is a supplemental registration form used to correct an error or amplify the information in the initial registration application form after it has been filed with the Copyright Office or a registration has been issued by the Copyright Office.

- *Form GR/CP* is a form used as an addition to a basic application on Form TX, Form PA, or Form VA if you are making a single registration for a group of contributions to periodicals. The copyright statute provides that a single registration for a group of works can be made if all of the following conditions are met: all of the works are by the same author, who is an individual; all of the works were first published as contributions to periodicals (including newspapers) within a twelve-month period; each of the contributions as first published bore a separate copyright notice and the name of the owner of copyright in the work was the same in each notice; one copy of the entire periodical issue or newspaper section in which each contribution was first published must be deposited with the application; and the application must identify each contribution separately, including the periodical containing it and the date of its first publication.

Use only the official Copyright Office application forms to apply for registration. The Copyright Office at one time refused to consider applications made on forms that were photocopied from the printed Copyright Office forms. In recent years, however, the Copyright Office has actually encouraged the use of such photocopied application forms. You may submit photocopied application forms so long as they are clear, legible, copied onto a good grade of white paper, and printed head-to-head, that is copied so that when you turn the sheet over, the top of the second page is directly behind the top of the first page. (Many local public libraries have a master set of copyright application forms available to be photocopied.) Because certificates of copyright registration are reproduced directly from the application forms filled out and submitted by applicants, the Copyright Office will reject any photocopied form that does not meet these requirements.

The Copyright Office also offers frequently requested Copyright Office registration applications, publications, and related materials via the Internet. These materials are available through the Copyright Office Home Page on the World Wide Web at *http://lcweb.loc.gov/ copyright*. There is no fee to connect to the Internet resources of the Copyright Office.

Registration Fees

Copyright registration is usually routinely granted by the Copyright Office and, in most cases, you can register your copyright yourself.

At this writing, registration costs twenty dollars per registration.

To avoid paying multiple registration fees, you may register the copyright in a collection of unpublished works for one fee, *if:*

- all the works in the collection were created by the same person or if one person is *an* author of all the works;
- all the works in the collection are owned by the same person;
- the works are bound together or otherwise assembled in an orderly form; and
- the collection of works is given a single title.

Many people use this method of registration to diminish copyright registration fees while gaining the advantages of copyright registration. Once each work is published, you should register it again, this time alone under its own title. Simply indicate on the new registration application in the appropriate blank that the single work was part of a previously registered collection of unpublished works.

Deposit Copies

Besides the registration fee, you must send the Copyright Office, in the same envelope with the registration fee, a non-returnable "deposit" (one or two copies of the work as specified by the Copyright Office according to the type of the work and whether it has been published and, if so, when), and a properly completed copyright registration form of the correct variety.

Information on Registration

The best way to figure out the requirements for any particular copyright registration is to order the free Copyright Office publications "Copyright Basics" and "Copyright Registration Procedures," as well as the pamphlet that explains registration procedures for the type of work you are registering (for example, "Copyright Registration for Works of the Visual Arts") when you order the appropriate registration form from the Copyright Office. Unless you already understand exactly what sort of deposit material you need to send with your application form, you can also ask the Copyright Office to send you a pamphlet or circular on the deposit required or permitted for your particular registration (for example, "Deposit Requirements for Claims to Copyright in Visual Arts Material"). If you read these simply written publications and follow the instruction sheet that comes attached to your registration form, you should be able to fill out the form correctly and submit the deposit copies necessary to register your copyright properly.

If after reading the pamphlets and the instruction sheet, you still have questions, you can call a Copyright Information Specialist at (202) 707-5959 for help. Information on ordering application forms and the Copyright Office publications mentioned above, as well as others, is given at the end of this chapter.

Benefits of Registration

Copyright registration is not required. The copyright statute automatically grants copyright protection to every work created on or after January 1, 1978, without requiring any action at all from the creator of the work before copyright protection begins. However, it is a very good idea to register the copyright in any work that you believe to be of more than passing significance, for several reasons.

Although it is not required for protection, copyright registration enhances the protection the statute grants automatically. Copyright registration is a prerequisite to filing a copyright infringement suit and "timely registration" makes it possible for the plaintiff in such a lawsuit to receive an award of statutory damages up to $100,000 and to recover his or her attorney fees and court costs. Both these possibilities make it much more feasible for a plaintiff to sue; in fact, many plaintiffs' claims of copyright infringement, though valid, may be all but unenforceable because the cost of bringing an infringement suit and financing it through the duration of the litigation is prohibitive—especially if the plaintiff must prove "actual damages" in court. (Actual damages are the amount of the plaintiff's losses because of the infringement plus the infringer's profits, as opposed to "statutory damages." Statutory damages are a range of money damages specified in the copyright statute that judges are allowed to award a plaintiff in a copyright infringement suit in lieu of "actual damages," the money actually lost by the plaintiff as a result of the defendant's infringing actions plus the actual amount by which the infringer profited from the use of the plaintiff's work. Awards of statutory damages are often desirable, for two reasons: because actual damages can be difficult, time-consuming, expensive, or impossible to prove during infringement lawsuits and because infringers often do not profit enough from their infringements to fund an adequate award to a prevailing plaintiff.)

Timely copyright registration is registration before the infringement occurs or, for published works, within three months of the date of publication (the date copies are offered without restriction to the public by sale or otherwise). Registration also gives notice to the world that the owner of the copyright claims ownership of the work that is registered and constitutes *prima facie* evidence in an infringement suit that the person who claims to own the copyright in the work is the legitimate copyright owner.

Equally important is the protection that registration provides if you are accused of having infringed someone else's copyright. Registration of your copyright establishes a public record that your copyrighted work existed in a certain form at least as early as the date of registration. This is all the proof necessary to prove that you are not guilty of infringement if the copyright you are accused of infringing was created later than yours—provided your work is still on deposit with the Copyright Office at the time of the lawsuit. Otherwise, if the two works are similar, proving your innocence can be difficult.

The flaw in this system is that, because of lack of storage space sufficient to warehouse for the full term of copyright copies of every work published in the United States, under ordinary circumstances, the Copyright Office will retain your deposit material for only five years. Because copyright infringement lawsuits must be filed within three years of the commission of the infringing act (or, in the case of a continuing infringement, three years from the date of the last infringing act), the ordinary retention period is sufficient in most cases to protect authors unjustly accused of infringement. You may request that the Copyright Office retain your deposit copies for the full term of copyright, but you must make written application for this service and pay $135 for the security it provides. If your work is very valuable or you expect that it may be the subject of litigation after the standard five-year retention period, it may be desirable to pay for full-term retention of a copy of your work. For specific information on how to arrange for full-term retention of your work, call a Copyright Information Specialist at (202) 707-5959.

Although it is best to register a copyright promptly, it's never too late to apply for registration. And if you make a mistake in filling out your registration form, the worst that will happen is that the Copyright Office will send it back to you with a letter specifying its inadequacy and requesting clarification. You will be given plenty of time to respond. Then, when the application is granted, you will be sent a certificate that gives for the effective date of your registration the date your application was first received by the Copyright Office. The vast majority of applications for copyright registration are granted, but if yours is denied for any reason, you will be sent a letter stating the basis for denial.

Mandatory Deposit for Published Works

Even if you do not register your copyright, the law requires you to "deposit" with the Copyright Office works published in the United States with notice of copyright. In general, the copyright owner or the owner of the exclusive right to publish the copyrighted work has a legal obligation to deposit two copies of the work for the use of the Library of Congress within three months of publication in the United States. Failure to do so does not invalidate copyright protection for the work but the law does prescribe fines and other penalties for failure to make this mandatory deposit.

The good news is that the deposit of copies you made with your copyright registration application completely satisfies the mandatory deposit requirements of the copyright statute. More good news is that Copyright Office regulations exempt certain categories of works entirely from the mandatory deposit requirements and reduce the requirements for other categories, such as certain works of the visual arts. The best way to make sense of this requirement with regard to any work that you publish but do not, for whatever reason, register, is to request the free publication "Mandatory Deposit of Copies or Phonorecords for the Library of Congress" from the Copyright Office. Information on ordering this pamphlet is given below.

Copyright Office Services

You may correspond with Copyright Office by writing: United States Copyright Office, Library of Congress, Washington, D.C. 20559.

The Copyright Office Public Information Office will give you general copyright information and will answer your questions about copyright registration. Recorded information is available twenty-four hours a day and seven days a week by calling (202) 707-3000.

You may speak to a Copyright Information Specialist by calling (202) 707-5959 between 8:30 A.M and 5:00 P.M. Monday through Friday (except holidays). (Copyright Information Specialists are knowledgeable and helpful, but the Copyright Office does not give legal advice and will not advise you regarding copyright infringement, bringing an infringement suit, or disputes over copyright ownership. You need a copyright lawyer for this sort of advice.) To write the Copyright Office Information Section, send your letter to: Information Section, LM-401, Copyright Office, Library of Congress, Washington, D.C. 20559.

The Copyright Forms Hotline

The Copyright Office will send you a supply of blank copyright registration forms free of charge if you call the Copyright Office Forms Hotline (twenty-four hours a day, every day) at (202) 707-9100. You can leave a recorded request on the Hotline answering machine specifying the forms you need; they'll show up in your mail in about two weeks.

Copyright Office Publications

The Copyright Office publishes a variety of excellent short pamphlets and circulars written in simple language on an assortment of copyright-related topics. A list of the most helpful of these publications, along with their corresponding publication numbers, follows.

You may order single copies of these publications by calling the Forms Hotline number or by writing the publications department of the Copyright Office: Information and Publications Section, LM-455, Copyright Office, Library of Congress, Washington, D.C. 20559.

PUBLICATION TITLE	PUBLICATION NUMBER

The Copyright Office has compiled information kits on a variety
of topics. Each kit contains all the Copyright Office publications and

registration forms that pertain to a particular sort of work. Like copyright registration forms or Copyright Office publications, these kits may be ordered by calling the Forms Hotline number or by writing the publications department of the Copyright Office: Information and Publications Section, LM-455, Copyright Office, Library of Congress, Washington, D.C. 20559.

PUBLICATION TITLE	KIT NUMBER
Fair Use	Kit 102
Music	Kit 105
Copyright Searches	Kit 116
Sound Recordings	Kit 121

Copyright Materials Via the Internet

The Copyright Office also offers frequently requested Copyright Office registration applications, publications, and related materials via the Internet. These materials are available through the Copyright Office Home Page on the World Wide Web at *http://lcweb.loc.gov/copyright.* There is no fee to connect to the Internet resources of the Copyright Office.

CHAPTER 5

Copyright Infringement

T HE ONLY THING worse than having to sue someone for copyright infringement is being sued yourself. If you create any sort of work—and especially if you license or assign your work to someone else or prepare it for an employer—you must know not only how to protect your own rights but also how to avoid trampling those of others. To determine whether your rights have been infringed or your work infringes someone else's work, you must first have a good understanding of what rights copyright gives to copyright owners. Only the person who created the copyrighted work (or someone to whom he or she has given permission to use the work) is legally permitted to reproduce, perform or display it, distribute copies of it, or create variations of it.

Defining Infringement

The federal copyright statute defines copyright infringement with a simple statement: "Anyone who violates any of the exclusive rights of [a] copyright owner . . . is an infringer of . . . copyright." Because it is a violation of rights granted under federal law, copyright infringement is actionable in federal court; that is, any copyright infringement lawsuit must be filed in one of the federal district courts distributed throughout the country.

The question of just *what* actions are sufficient to violate the rights of a copyright owner is left for courts to answer as they evaluate the circumstances in each case of claimed infringement. The body of law made up of court decisions in copyright infringement cases is called copyright "case law." Copyright case law is the source for the test for copyright infringement and the standard for applying the test to the facts in particular copyright infringement cases.

Although any of the exclusive rights of copyright may be infringed, as a practical matter, copyright infringement suits usually claim that the defendant copied the plaintiff's work without permission. Sometimes an infringer *has* intentionally copied the copyright owner's song or book or painting in an effort to steal the successful features of that work and profit from them. However, many copyright infringement lawsuits are brought because the plaintiff wrongly believes that someone who has created a *somewhat* similar work has infringed the plaintiff's copyright by copying. Understanding copyright infringement means understanding the standard courts use in evaluating whether accusations of copyright infringement are true.

The Infringement Test

Assuming that the copyright in the work that is said to have been infringed is valid and that the work was created *before* the work accused of infringing it, and in the absence of any admission by the defendant author that he or she *did* copy the plaintiff's work, courts ordinarily judge copyright infringement by a circumstantial evidence test.

The circumstantial evidence test for copyright infringement has three parts:

1. Did the accused infringer have *access* to the work that is said to have been infringed, so that copying was possible?

2. Is the defendant actually guilty of *copying* part of the plaintiff's protectable expression from the plaintiff's work?
3. Is the accused work *substantially similar* to the work the plaintiff says was copied?

If you can remember and understand these three parts of the test for copyright infringement, "access," "copying," and "substantial similarity," you should always be able to decide correctly for yourself whether a work of yours infringes someone else's work or whether someone else has infringed your copyright.

Access to the "Infringed" Work

"Access" simply means what it says. Did the accused infringer have access to the "infringed" work before creating the "infringing" work? It's very important to remember that the action for which the copyright statute prescribes penalties is *copying,* not the mere *coincidental creation* of a work that is similar or even nearly identical to a pre-existing work. In most cases, access is not presumed but must be proved before the questions of copying and substantial similarity even enter the equation.

This means that if you write a piece for a banking trade magazine on the continuing economic fallout from the epidemic of savings and loan association failures in the past decade and some journalist on the other side of the continent writes an article on the same subject for an issue of *Business Week* that hits the newsstands only days after your piece is published, *each* of you owns a valid copyright in your own article, even if the *Business Week* article addresses all the same issues as yours does and comes to the exact same conclusions.

This is easier to understand if you remember that our copyright statute rewards the act of creation. You own the copyright in a product of your own imagination so long as your imagination—and not that of another author—really is the source of your work. This is true regardless of what anybody else in the world comes up with before, at the same time as, or after you create your work.

If you are a freelancer, the obvious implication of the access requirement in proving copyright infringement is that good documentation of your attempts to sell your novel or song or screenplay to those who are in position to exploit them can be critically important in the event someone decides your work is good enough to steal. If you know where your manuscript or demo tape or script has been, you may be able to prove that an infringer had "reasonable opportunity" (which is usually sufficient proof of access) to copy your work.

Copying of Protectable Expression

The circumstantial evidence test for copyright infringement is like a three-legged stool. All three legs of the test are necessary to support a claim of copyright infringement, and the absence of proof of one of the three parts of the test means an infringement suit will fail. Proving the second element of copyright infringement, copying of protected subject matter, is just as important as proving access and substantial similarity, but would-be plaintiffs often gloss over this requirement in the mistaken assumption that *any* copying is sufficient to support an infringement suit.

To understand what constitutes copying of protected expression, you must consider what elements of your work are not protected. The copyright statute specifically excludes from protection "any idea, procedure, process, system, method of operation, concept, principle or discovery." And, as we discussed in chapter 1, there are several categories of elements of copyrightable works, some of them important to the overall quality of a work, that are not protected by copyright.

If you review the list of *exceptions* to the general rule that copyright protects what you create, you can better apply the second part of the test for copyright infringement. It is: *Does the material suspected to have been copied from the "infringed" work include protectable expression?* If your answer is "yes" and it can be proved that the accused infringer had access to the work that is said to have been infringed, you must then evaluate whether the theft was substantial.

Substantial Similarity

The third part of the test for copyright infringement is determining whether the "infringing" work is "substantially similar" to the "infringed" work. Substantial similarity is hard to define. Even the courts have never been able to come up with a hard-and-fast test for determining substantial similarity. This may be because no such test is possible; each copyright infringement case must be decided entirely on the facts of *that* case, and what happened in a similar suit has no real bearing on the question whether *this* defendant did create a work that is substantially similar to that of *this* plaintiff. The test for copyright infringement is like the system one Supreme Court justice once said he used for determining whether a work was obscene, "I can't define it," he said, "but I know it if I see it."

Although it's not possible to pinpoint the border between infringing and non-infringing similarity, a map of the danger zone between the two exists in the form of copyright case law. Courts do not require plaintiffs to demonstrate that their defendants' works are nearly identical to their own works to prove substantial similarity. However, courts will not interpret even several small, unimportant similarities between the works in question as substantial similarity. In short, "substantial similarity" is just that: substantial. The *sort* of similarity between two works is just as important as the *degree* of similarity—the judgment of substantial similarity is both *qualitative* and *quantitative.*

Further, although plaintiffs in copyright infringement suits routinely hire expert witnesses—usually people who are very familiar with the sort of work that is the subject of litigation—to testify as to what similarities exist between the works at issue, courts judge whether those similarities are substantial by the "ordinary observer" test, which is a sort of "man on the street" view of the effect of those similarities. Courts try to decide whether an ordinary observer, reading or hearing or seeing two similar works for the first time, would believe that the "infringing" work and "infringed" work are the same. If so, substantial similarity exists. This means that you probably have the equipment you need—your own eyes and ears—to decide for yourself whether someone's work infringes yours.

Examples of Substantial Similarity

Some examples of actions that will always result in infringement if the work copied is not a public domain work will help you grasp the difficult concept of substantial similarity.

Outright duplication of significant portions of a work obviously results in substantial similarity; this sort of substantial similarity has been characterized as taking the fundamental substance of another's work and is the sort of copying that is often simply called "plagiarism."

Another sort of substantial similarity has been called "comprehensive literal similarity." This occurs when, as a whole, the accused work tracks the pattern of expression of the work said to have been infringed and uses the same theme or format. Close paraphrasing of an entire protected work or significant portions of it would produce this variety of substantial similarity.

A third variety of substantial similarity is the taking of portions of a work that are important to the impact and character of the work from which they are taken but which do not amount to a large portion of the infringing work. This sort of infringing substantial similarity points up the fact that what is important is the quantity and importance of the material taken from the infringed work rather than simply the portion of the infringing work that the stolen material constitutes. In other words, an infringer cannot escape responsibility for his or her infringing actions by pointing out how much of the infringing work was *not* stolen.

Striking Similarity

There is one situation in which one part of the three-part test for copyright infringement need not be proved. That is the situation in which there is "striking similarity" between two works. Essentially, this is just a specialized application of the three-part infringement test. In cases where the similarity between the two works at issue is so striking that there's no explanation for such overwhelming similarity other than that one work was copied from the other, courts say that access may be assumed and the circumstances that made the infringement possible need not be reconstructed by the plaintiff. The "striking similarity" approach to proving infringement is rarely allowed by courts, which prefer to see plaintiffs prove every element of their cases.

Creator Beware

Copyright infringement is an area of real danger for creative people. Consequently, anyone who aspires to earn a living by exploiting the products of his or her imagination needs to know enough about copyright infringement to stay out of danger. People only think that writing plays or songs or advertising copy is a nice, safe job that can't get anyone in trouble. In reality, what you do with your typewriter or guitar or pad and pencil in your own little workspace can land you in federal court, where you will be asked to explain just *what* you did and *why* and *when* you did it.

If You Want to Be a Plaintiff

If you think someone has infringed your copyright, see a lawyer who's well-versed in copyright law. Most lawyers will not charge you for an initial consultation about a possible copyright infringement case. You'll need the objective evaluation an experienced lawyer can give you, since creative people are notoriously poor judges of whether their works have actually been infringed. Your lawyer should be willing to tell you whether there has been an infringement and, if so, whether you're likely to prevail in court. If you don't like what the first lawyer you consult says, make an appointment with another for a second evaluation.

Because the "statute of limitations" (the period within which you must file suit) for copyright infringement is only three years from the date the infringer commits the infringing acts, don't wait too long before you take your suspicions of infringement to a lawyer. (In the case of a continuing infringement, such as printing a large number of copies of a pirated book over a period of time, the statute runs from the date of the defendant's last infringing act.) After three years your infringement suit may be barred. That is, the court will throw it out because you did not file it within the prescribed three-year period. You snooze, you lose.

If you win your copyright infringement suit, the court may issue a permanent injunction that prohibits any further use of the work that violates your copyright. It may order the seizure and destruction of any copies of the infringing work. It may award you "actual damages" (the profits the infringer made from the infringing work and the money you lost because of the infringement) or, alternately, "statutory damages" (a range of money damages the court is allowed to award you in lieu of actual damages), the expenses of the suit that you've had to pay, and attorneys' fees.

Defenses to Infringement

As in any civil or criminal litigation, the defendant in a copyright infringement suit may offer various arguments to demonstrate either that his or her actions did not infringe the plaintiff's work or, if they did, that there are good reasons why the court should not punish him or her. These arguments that a defendant makes in self-defense are called "defenses." Many defenses to charges of copyright infringement are technical in nature. Others are rarely used. By far, the most important and the most commonly used of such defenses is the defense of "fair use."

Fair Use

There are situations in which you may use parts of another person's copyrighted work without that person's permission and without infringing that person's copyright. This sort of use is called "fair use." The fair use defense can render otherwise infringing actions non-infringing.

Fair use is a kind of public policy exception to the usual standard for determining copyright infringement; that is, there is an infringing use of a copyrighted work, but because of a countervailing public interest, that use is permitted and is not called infringement. Any use that is deemed by the law to be "fair" typically creates some social, cultural, or political benefit which outweighs any resulting harm to the copyright owner.

Courts consider a long list of factors in determining whether a use is "fair." The copyright statute identifies six purposes that will qualify a use as a possible fair use. They are uses made for the purpose of "criticism, comment, news reporting, teaching (including multiple copies for classroom use), scholarship, or research." Once any use of a copyrighted work has met this threshold test, that is, has been proved to have been made for one of these six purposes permitted in the statute, the use must be examined to determine whether it is indeed fair.

The copyright statute lists four factors that courts must weigh in determining fair use. They are:

1. The purpose and character of the use, including whether such use is of a commercial nature or is for non-profit educational purposes; [Educational, research, criticism, and news reporting uses are almost always fair; commercial uses, such as uses in advertising, are seldom fair uses.]

2. The nature of the copyrighted work; [The permissible uses that may be made of informational works are considerably broader than permissible uses of creative works. However, courts have yet to permit the fair use defense to infringement in a case involving an *unpublished* work, where the private nature of the work is ordinarily protected.]

3. The amount and substantiality of the portion used in relation to the copyrighted work as a whole; and [This is the "substantial similarity" question again. It is quantitative and qualitative; that is, did you quote the twelve-page climactic scene of a mystery novel, thereby disclosing the identity of the killer, or did you quote only a three-paragraph section that describes the city where the detective works?]

4. The effect of the use upon the potential market for or value of the copyrighted work. [This evaluation is often determinative in a court's decision whether the use constitutes infringement. It is undoubtedly the most important of the four factors to be weighed in determining fair use. If the market for the copyrighted work is significantly diminished because of the purported fair use, then it is not a fair use. Fewer readers will want to buy a book if its most sensational and newsworthy sections have been previously excerpted in a magazine. A related factor that is considered is the effect of the purported fair use on any of the rights in the copyright of the work said to be infringed.

If, without permission, one person writes and sells a screen-play based on another person's copyrighted novel, the right to prepare and sell a screen adaptation of the novel may have been lost to the author of that novel.]

The House Report that accompanied the 1976 Copyright Act is informative because it illustrates the scope of the fair use section of the statute with several examples of fair use:

Quotation of excerpts in a review or criticism for purposes of illustration or comment; quotation of short passages in a scholarly or technical work, for illustration or clarification of the author's observations; use in a parody of some of the content of the work parodied; summary of an address or article, with brief quotations, in a news report; reproduction by a library of a portion of a work to replace part of a damaged copy; reproduction by a teacher or student of a small part of a work to illustrate a lesson; reproduction of a work in legislative or judicial proceedings or reports; incidental and fortuitous reproduction, in a newsreel or broadcast, of a work located in the scene of an event being reported.

Avoiding Claims of Infringement

Whenever you encounter or consider using someone else's work, take care that any use of a copyrighted work falls into one of the fair use exceptions to infringement and take action to protect yourself from false claims of infringement. Creators and business people who deal in creative works can greatly diminish the like-lihood of being sued for copyright infringement by using the simple techniques outlined below.

1. Keep your notes and the progressive drafts or sketches, etc. of your creative work to prove that you created your work yourself. Date each such document when you create it in the same pen or pencil, etc. used to write or draw the draft of your work. If you do not own the books, etc. that you referred to in the process of creating your work, make sure you keep a list of any such works you used for reference to show where you got your information.

2. Parody of copyrighted works is not a permissible fair use

unless the parody uses only so much of the parodied work as is necessary to "call to mind" the parodied work; this is dangerous to attempt without very careful attention to the question of infringement. Anyone who must use more than a small segment or feature of a copyrighted work to make a parody of that work effective should consider approaching the owner of the copyright in the work for permission to use whatever portion of the work is necessary.

3. If you are an editor or publisher, a movie producer or director, a music publisher, a writer, an artist, a songwriter, a screenwriter, a copywriter, or are in any position or profession that involves the exploitation or creation of copyrighted works, be careful what you are exposed to. Promptly return manuscripts, scripts, songs, etc. submitted to you for possible use if you cannot use them. Keep a record of what and when and to whom such materials are returned. Consider refusing to examine any such material at all until it is registered for copyright, especially if it is unpublished, or without a release of liability from the creator. If you are a creator of copyrights, and especially if you are successful in your field, protect yourself from people who want to show you their newest work, especially if they are unknown to you. Disappointed and envious creators have been known to sue those who enjoy more success in the mistaken belief that part of that success originated with themselves.

4. Direct quotations should always be attributed. Quotations of short passages of copyrighted works, such as the sort of quoting found in book reviews or news stories, is generally safe in any context where the First Amendment protection of free speech can be reasonably invoked, even if the piece in which the quotation is used has a partially commercial purpose. You should also attribute closely paraphrased statements. It is very important to understand, however, that you cannot escape responsibility for copyright infringement simply by attributing the lifted portion of any work to its author; if the "borrowed" segment amounts to a substantial portion of the copyrighted work, attribution does not eradicate your sin. As indicated earlier, you should also avoid any use of even two-

or three-paragraph direct quotations or close paraphrases if they embody the "meat" of the work from which they were taken or if use of them would diminish the salability of that work. And if you do paraphrase another writer's work, attribute the ideas you use to the other writer. Do your homework; use as many sources as are available for your work. Remember the old saw that "stealing from one source is plagiarism, but stealing from several sources is research."

5. Working journalists and people affiliated with non-profit institutions such as schools and churches have more latitude in using other people's copyrighted works than the average painter or writer or composer. A professor who duplicates a poem to use as a handout in an English class is probably not going to run afoul of the copyright owner of the poem. However, Kinko's encountered big trouble, in the form of a lawsuit for copyright infringement, when it disregarded this principle of the law of fair use. Without permission from the copyright holders, Kinko's was assembling from many sources "anthologies" consisting of writings taught in university courses and selling them to students. These makeshift anthologies hurt the market for the books that legitimately contained the copied writings. Kinko's lost the suit; it has been remarkably attentive to the interests of copyright holders since.

6. Obtain permission to use any photo, letter, passage, illustration, etc. that is either unpublished or, if previously published, is possibly still protected by copyright. Save the permissions you obtain in a file. Never exceed the permission granted and never use any material for which permission to use has been denied. (A form permission letter appears in the Appendix to this book.) And remember that using unpublished works without permission is especially dangerous, even if the use is minimal. A tension exists between the owners of such materials and biographers, historians, and other scholars who may want to quote from them. It is understandable that anyone who needs to reproduce in a biography or journal article long passages from the unpublished letters or manuscripts of his or her subject would dislike this restriction. However, the law protects the privacy of those who do not wish to make their

writings public and does not require the owners of those copyrights to pay any attention at all to even the most valid requests for permission to reproduce and publish such works. Presently, only the most narrow uses may be made of unpublished works without the consent of the owner of copyright in them and disregarding restrictions placed on the use of unpublished materials is dangerous. Even close paraphrasing of such materials may be actionable.

If You Find Yourself a Defendant

In determining whether your work infringes someone else's copyright, let your conscience be your guide; if you think that you have taken more than inspiration from another, copyrighted, work, you could very well have stepped over the meandering boundary between permissible use of another's work and "substantial similarity."

If someone sues you for copyright infringement and is able to prove to the court that an infringement took place, that copyright owner may obtain an injunction to halt further sales, distribution or dissemination of the infringing work; you could also be forced to pay a substantial judgment, including any profits you have made from the infringement and, possibly, the attorneys' fees and costs of the successful plaintiff. The lawyers' fees incurred in defending through trial a copyright infringement suit can be, in themselves, enormous, even if the judgment is not. And even if the case is settled before it goes to trial, you still may have to pay a cash settlement to the plaintiff, as well as your lawyer's fees for handling the case to the point of settlement. Finding yourself on the receiving end of these remedies for infringement will make you regret that you were ever so foolish as to trifle with the copyright of the plaintiff.

Is It Infringement?

1. You want to use Grant Wood's famous painting *American Gothic* in a magazine ad for your travel agency ("Bored At Home?"), so you shoot a copy of it from an Art Institute of Chicago guidebook, blow it up a little, add copy, and run the ad in the travel section of the Sunday paper. Is it infringement?

Yes. You are in double trouble with this ad. Grant Wood painted *American Gothic* in 1930. Although he died in 1942, the copyright in the painting, which will endure through the end of 2005 if it was renewed after the first twenty-eight-year term of copyright protection, is owned by his estate. Not only did you not have the right to use Wood's painting without permission, you also did not have the right to copy the photograph of the painting. The Art Institute of Chicago owns the copyright in that photograph and your copying the photo without permission constitutes a second infringement of copyright. (See chapter 3 for a more detailed discussion of the duration of copyright in older works.)

2. Your boss put you in charge of writing the sales training manual that will be sent out to all the branch offices of your company. You are a fan of Mark McCormack's book *What They Don't Teach You at Harvard Business School* and decide to "paraphrase" two chapters of this bestseller as sections of your training manual. You proudly present the finished manual to your boss, who takes it home to read over the weekend. You are chagrined and surprised when he demands to see you first thing Monday morning. It seems that your boss is also a fan of Mr. McCormack and has recognized the source material for the two "paraphrased" sections of the manual. He says that you and your company could be sued by McCormack and his publisher. You are almost sure that paraphrasing McCormack's material is all it takes to eliminate the threat of any lawsuit. Is it infringement?

Yes, of the most blatant sort. While it is permissible to quote authorities in any field ("McCormack believes that . . .") or even to cite their theories without attribution ("Many business theorists hold that . . ."), use of whole chunks of their writings is a violation of their rights and the rights of their publishers, to whom they have assigned the exclusive right to reproduce and disseminate their works. When you "paraphrased" Mr. McCormack's chapters, you followed them line by line and simply changed the way his ideas were expressed. While no one's *ideas* are protected by copyright, their expressions are protected. Your paraphrasing was a bodily theft of Mr. McCormack's expressions of his ideas. The fact that you changed Mr. McCormack's words makes little difference since the sections of your training manual based on his chapters are simply reworded duplications of his statements. That's copying of protected expression. *And* substantial similarity. Your boss is also right that both you *and* your employer can be sued for copyright infringement. As a full-time employee, you are an agent of your company. Any action that you take during the course of performing your duties as an employee is attributable to your company. Your boss is one smart guy. Maybe that's why he's the boss. Next time, if you can't come up with your own material, either hire someone on a work-for-hire basis to write your manual or copy *The Prince* by Niccolo Machiavelli, written in 1513, or *The Art of War* by Sun Tzu, written more than 2,500 years ago. But stay strictly away from the work of anyone who ever saw an electric lightbulb.

3. You reprint the entire text of Martin Luther King, Jr.'s famous "I Have a Dream" speech on "parchment" paper in a form suitable for framing for your alma mater, a small and struggling but well-regarded liberal arts college, which sells the printed speeches for ten dollars each to raise money for a new library. Is it infringement?

    Almost certainly. Any use of the full text for Dr. King's 1960's speech without the permission of his estate constitutes infringement, especially if that use is made for commercial gain, as in this situation. It is possible that you could successfully argue that your otherwise infringing use of the speech is actually a "fair use" because it was made on behalf of and for the benefit of a non-profit educational institution, but it is more likely that a court would, at the very least, require your college to pay a royalty on each copy of the King speech sold. The King estate could also ask the court to stop the sale of the speech, to compel the destruction of all unsold copies of it, and to make your *alma mater* pay it the profits from all sales made. Even national heroes have copyright rights.

4. On the cover of your corporation's annual report, you use a

photo of a small segment of a *Wall Street Journal* article that contains a twenty-five-word quotation naming your corporation as an innovator in its field. Is it infringement?

No. Your use of the *Wall Street Journal* quotation is a fair use of that publication's copyrighted story in two ways; it is a properly attributed short quote used in a First Amendment context, since the annual report is the corporation's way of informing its stockholders about the corporation, and you used only a small portion of the *Journal* story, not enough to constitute "substantial similarity" between the text of the annual report and the *Journal* story. Reprinting the whole story without permission for distribution to stockholders would be a different matter.

5. You own an auto dealership and advertise yourself as "The Super-Dealer." In your newest ads, which you dreamed up yourself, you use a photo of yourself dressed in blue long johns, a red cape, and a wide gold belt, standing shoulder-to-shoulder with those other superheroes, Batman and Superman, who appear as their original cartoon-figure, comic-book selves. Is it infringement?

Yes, two kinds. You infringed the copyright rights of the publishers from whose comic books you copied the cartoon figures you used and you infringed their trademark rights by using the well-known superheroes to attract attention to your ads. You are in more trouble for your trademark transgression than for your copyright infringement. Duck into a phone booth and disguise yourself as a smarter person.

6. Armed with a brand-new diploma in hotel-restaurant management, you go to work for your Uncle Vito, helping him run his restaurant, Vito's. Driving to the restaurant on your second day of work, you hear on your favorite oldies station the Billy Joel standard "My Italian Restaurant." You get the great idea to use the song as the background for the new radio and television spots you talked your uncle into the day before. You buy a copy of the Billy Joel album that includes "My Italian Restaurant," get your uncle to narrate the spots, and rush to get them on the air. Your uncle loves the spots and you begin to think about asking for a raise. Then one morning your uncle receives by

certified mail a "cease and desist letter" from a New York law firm representing Billy Joel's record company and music publishing company. The letter informs your uncle that his use of the Billy Joel recording of the song "My Italian Restaurant" in ads for Vito's is an infringement of the copyright rights of both the record company, which owns the copyright in the recording of the song, and the music publishing company, which owns the copyright in the song itself. Your uncle calls you and wakes you up to ask "Is it infringement?"

Yes. The New York lawyers are right. They demand that your Uncle Vito immediately "cease" use of the recording or song and "desist" from any additional use of either and offer to forego filing suit if your uncle pays a settlement of $10,000 within thirty days, in lieu of the licensing fees they would have charged had he contacted them before using the song and recording. The lawyer you and your uncle consult brushes aside your arguments that, since no more than sixty seconds of the recording were used in any spot, your use of the song and recording does not constitute infringement and that, in any event, your uncle shouldn't be sued, since neither you nor he *intended* to trespass on anyone's rights. He says that any broadcast of any recording of a copyrighted song in a *commercial* context is infringement if it is made without the permission of the owners of the copyrights in the recording and in the song because it is a violation of the copyright owners' exclusive right to control performances of their copyrighted recording and song. He says that using sixty seconds or thirty seconds or even ten seconds of a three-minute recording is more than sufficient to eliminate any argument that Vito's use of "My Italian Restaurant" was merely an incidental, "fair" use of the song and recording. He tells you that it is immaterial that you did not realize that your actions amounted to infringement, since copyright infringement is judged by evaluating the quantity, quality, and context of the use of the copyrighted work, *not* by gauging the wrongful intent of the accused infringer. When you make your brilliant argument that you know for a fact (because you once had a summer job as a deejay) that radio stations do not call up record companies and music publishing companies to ask permission before playing each recording they broadcast, your lawyer reminds you that radio stations (and other users of copyrighted recordings) pay license fees each year to the performing rights organizations that collect such fees on behalf of songwriters and publishers. Uncle Vito settles. You are out of bright ideas. And out of a job.

CHAPTER 6

The Perils of Litigation

PEOPLE WHO BELIEVE that their copyrights have been infringed often have no idea how complicated copyright infringement lawsuits are and exaggerated ideas about how much money they can recover if they bring suit against the suspected infringer. Unfortunately, the unwarranted contemplation of the large amounts of money one feels certain he or she will be awarded is often the most satisfying stage of a copyright infringement suit. As with most civil litigation, copyright infringement suits are more fun for plaintiffs to think about than participate in. For defendants, lawsuits are no fun at all.

Every ancient mapmaker knew that his very own country was the center of the world, but most were confused as to what lay over the horizon. They prudently decided that what they didn't know could hurt them and often marked these vast *terra incognita* areas with the warning "Heere Bee Dragons" to warn explorers of the perils there. If you have never been involved in a civil lawsuit, this is a wise attitude to cultivate toward suing and being sued, because today in the United States the dragons are Litigants and Lawyers.

This doesn't mean that there are no issues worth going to court over—litigation is sometimes the only way to settle some disputes or pursue that elusive goal, justice. However, and especially with regard to business disputes of any sort, litigation should be viewed as a last resort. In civilized countries, if your neighbor offends you, you do not engage him and his clan in a feud. Rather, you file your complaint in a court of law and let a judge decide the dispute. Unfortunately, the U.S. judicial system is so complex that a lawsuit can leave you as bloodied as a fistfight; even if you win you are bruised by the experience.

Lawyers

If you decide to sue someone for copyright infringement, the first thing you must do is find an experienced copyright litigator to represent you. In Great Britain, lawyers are classified as either "barristers," that is, lawyers who represent clients in court, or "solicitors," lawyers who counsel clients concerning every sort of legal matter, including lawsuits, but who do not represent clients in court. In the United States, there is no such formal division among lawyers, but most lawyers consider themselves primarily either counselors or litigators. If you have an established relationship with a lawyer you trust, it is probably a good idea to ask that lawyer to refer you to a copyright lawyer for evaluation of the merits of your claim.

Deciding whether you have a real case is not a determination you should try to make yourself, even *after* reading this book. A competent evaluation of whether to bring suit in a suspected case of copyright infringement involves a careful analysis of the question of whether the suspect actions actually *do* constitute copyright infringement. For this evaluation, only a lawyer who is well-versed in copyright law can reliably advise you.

Copyright lawyers tend to be few and far between in some areas of the country. If your own lawyer can't refer you to a copyright lawyer he or she knows personally, the best way to find a good one may be to call Volunteer Lawyers for the Arts. Volunteer Lawyers for the Arts (VLA) is a legal aid organization for creative people and arts organizations. If you live in the New York area, the VLA staff or a volunteer attorney may be able to help you. Their address and phone number are: Volunteer Lawyers for the Arts, 1 East 53rd Street, New York, NY 10022, (212) 319-2787. If you don't live near New York, call the VLA Art Law Line, (212) 319-2910, for referral to the nearest of the more than forty other volunteer lawyers for the arts organizations that exist around the country.

Another very good way to find a lawyer capable of handling your copyright case is to consult a trade organization that promotes the interests of people in your industry or profession. For example, the American Society of Media Photographers maintains a good list of lawyers around the country who are experienced in copyright litigation. Most other similar organizations also collect similar information for member referrals. If you inquire and there is no formal list of lawyers for referral purposes, try to talk to the executive director of the organization. He or she almost certainly will be able to give you some names of lawyers experienced in lawsuits similar to yours and may even be willing to confidentially evaluate the relative merits of the lawyers recommended.

Responsible lawyers will not bring frivolous suits on your behalf; a lawyer has an ethical duty to determine that any lawsuit he or she files for you is founded on a reasonable interpretation of the law, and that your allegations against your defendant are based in fact and are not merely unfounded claims. However, no lawyer can guarantee the outcome of any suit. The best your lawyer can do is make a prediction of your chances of prevailing based on her or his interpretation of the copyright statute and the precedents set by court decisions in similar cases.

Remember, your lawsuit is brought in *your* name, not your lawyer's; your lawyer is only a skilled agent acting on your behalf. It is *your* testimony that will be required, and you who stand to gain from any judgment in your favor. And it is *you* who will be footing the bill for all the work your attorney must perform to represent you adequately.

Lawyers' Fees

Lawyers' fees run from a low of around $75 per hour to $300 per hour or more in some cities. What your lawsuit will cost, in attorneys' fees and costs such as court filing fees, costs of court reports for depositions, expert witness fees, etc., depends mostly on how complicated the issues in your case are, how many people are involved, how well-financed they are, how vigorously they defend against your claims, and whether the suit must be brought in another city or can be filed where you live.

However, even a relatively uncomplicated suit can cost you several thousand dollars to bring to the point of trial. Complicated lawsuits involving multiple plaintiffs and/or defendants are a litigator's dream; despite his or her best efforts to bring the suit to a quick resolution, the legal work involved may produce fat fees for several years.

And although most clients who have been through an expensive lawsuit would hesitate to admit it, there's nothing unfair about a lawyer charging for his or her work. If anything is unfair about a lawsuit, it is the fact that circumstances compel you to be involved in one in the first place. All your lawyer can do is use every tactic at his or her disposal to get you out of it as soon as possible.

Sometimes lawyers will agree to represent clients in lawsuits on a "contingency fee" basis. This means that the lawyer will represent the client without payment for her or his services during the course of the lawsuit for a large share, usually one-third, of any sum eventually awarded the client by the court.

Before accepting any case on this basis, a lawyer will look at the amount of legal work involved, the probable amount of damages that could be awarded, and the likelihood that the plaintiff will win the suit. This is because a lawyer who has accepted a case on this basis earns nothing in return for sometimes literally years of work if the court rules against her or his client. And bringing a suit even on a contingency fee basis can still be expensive for the client, since the client may have to pay all the expenses of the suit, which can be considerable.

Persuading a good copyright lawyer to take your case on a contingency fee basis may depend on the size of the pot of gold at the end of the lawsuit, rather than the merits of your claim. If you have difficulty getting a big-gun lawyer to take your case on a contingency fee basis, look for a younger lawyer who, although possibly less experienced, will perhaps be more eager to earn his or her spurs as a copyright litigator.

Another important question that must be answered before your lawyer will begin chasing an infringer on your behalf is that of the terms of the agreement you and your lawyer make concerning fees. It is customary that a lawyer working on a contingency fee basis will expect to be paid one-third of any recovery that his or her client makes, whether that recovery results from a settlement fee or an award of damages by a court. However, it is important to inquire whether the expenses of the suit are to be subtracted from the total recovery amount *before* or *after* your lawyer's fee is calculated. This is a bargaining chip. If you are fortunate enough to have caught a deep-pocket infringer red-handed, your lawyer will look more favorably on a proposal that his or her firm advance the costs of your suit, with the understanding that the firm will be repaid when you win the suit. Expect that your lawyer will ask you to sign a written fee agreement before beginning work, even if *you* must pay all the expenses connected with the suit. This is only good business. However, get another lawyer to review the terms of the fee agreement if you do not fully understand them, especially if you believe your suit could produce a large cash settlement or award of damages.

Client Misconceptions

If more people had fewer assumptions about lawsuits and the judicial process, the public image of lawyers as a group would be better. Clients somehow believe in their hearts that their lawyers can control the outcome of lawsuits and very often become disenchanted with their own lawyers, not to mention the lawyers of their adversaries, if they lose their suits. Judges decide cases based on laws passed by legislators who were elected by you. Lawyers are like guides through what is today in the United States often a legal jungle; they are stuck with the laws and the judges they encounter and must do their best to guide you through the litigation process, but cannot change the basic rules by which the litigation must be conducted.

Nevertheless, clients think, on some level, that all a lawyer has to do is reach into the bottom drawer of his or her desk, fill out a form marked "Lawsuit," file it at the courthouse and—voilà!—the worthless human being who has just been labeled the "Defendant" will be hauled to a cell under the courthouse that very afternoon by two or more burly federal marshals.

Unfortunately, it doesn't happen that way. You may know that your defendant is dead wrong and a sneaky, dishonest person besides, and the defendant may know it, too, but before the *court* knows it, you have to *prove* it, while simultaneously fighting the best efforts of the defendant to avoid admitting that he did anything wrong. That's why your lawyer will plot your lawsuit like a chess game and view the trial as a battle.

The Course of a Lawsuit

Litigation is a long process, and in real life, most of it takes place before the trial. The first thing your lawyer will do after investigating the facts surrounding your grievance against your adversary and the law governing your claim is to draft what is called your "complaint." A complaint is a carefully worded document that sets out the facts of your dispute, relates them to the law, tells how the defendant has transgressed your rights under the law, and asks for certain "relief," from and on account of the defendant's transgressions, such as an injunction (an order from the court directing the defendant to do something or to stop doing something) or an award of damages (money awarded to compensate you for your losses or punish the defendant).

Plaintiffs should know that lawyers always ask for more than they have any hope of actually receiving; those "Million Dollar Lawsuit" headlines you see may result, long after the newsprint has faded, in actual awards of only a few thousand dollars, which may be barely enough to cover the legal fees of the plaintiffs.

The lawsuit officially begins when your complaint is filed with the court. After the defendant is formally notified of the suit, he or she has a specified period of time within which to file an "answer" with the court that responds to each allegation made in the complaint, giving the defendant's side of the matter.

In many suits, before and sometimes also after the answer is filed, the defendant will file various motions objecting to one or another important procedural aspect of the lawsuit in an effort to have the case dismissed, or, at least, to delay its progress. Your lawyer must file a response challenging any such motion and must support your position with a written "brief," which is a concise statement of the law and facts relating to the issue raised in the defendant's motion and which is meant to educate the judge and persuade him or her that the defendant's motion should not be granted. These motions, each countered by well-researched and carefully written briefs, can continue for a frustratingly long time.

Meanwhile, another interesting and, for the lawyers, often lucrative part of the lawsuit is going on; this is "discovery," the minuet between the parties to the suit by which each litigant "discovers" from the other as many facts as possible related to the lawsuit. Discovery tools include interrogatories (written questions), requests for production of documents (written requests for pertinent paperwork), and depositions (oral testimony taken out of court, but under oath and recorded by a court reporter). Discovery can also take forever.

Once the complaint and answer are filed, all the motions are made, answered, and ruled on by the court, and discovery is complete, the case can be set for trial. Both your lawyer and the defendant's lawyer will pore over all the facts they've gathered, assess the strengths of their arguments, and map out their plans to present those facts and arguments in court before the judge, if the trial is to be a "bench trial," or the jury.

Experts

One of the people who you may be hiring at exorbitant rates is someone called an "expert witness." Expert witnesses in copyright infringement cases may testify to prove several issues, such as: the originality of the copyrighted work; whether the defendant copied from the copyrighted work; whether the copied material constitutes protectable expression; whether audiences will perceive substantial similarity between the plaintiff's work and the defendant's work; the effect of the defendant's use on the marketability of the plaintiff's work; and the portion of the defendant's profits from the infringement that is due the plaintiff. Such testimony can be especially important in cases involving computer programs, where similarity between the works at issue cannot be judged by ordinary people. For example, the opinion of an expert may be necessary to determine whether the defendant tried to conceal the fact that his or her computer program was copied from the plaintiff's program by translating it into another computer language.

Settlement

A very large percentage of lawsuits are settled just prior to trial, sometimes literally in the hallway outside the courtroom just before the proceedings are to begin. This is because no one, least of all lawyers, wants to go through a trial if a settlement is offered on any basis that is at all acceptable. Even more persuasive is the attitude of most judges, who actively encourage settlements to reduce their heavy workload, to save taxpayers' money, and to clear perpetually clogged court dockets.

A settlement agreement between the litigants also usually eliminates the possibility that the lawsuit isn't over even after the fat lady sings. Many losing litigants can find reasons to appeal the judgments entered against them by their trial courts. Sometimes a litigant will appeal up the ladder of courts more than once, on one ground or another, until all the people involved in the original lawsuit feel that they have unwittingly wandered into Charles Dickens's famous never-ending fictional lawsuit, *Jarndyce v. Jarndyce.*

Plaintiff Versus Defendant

The only thing worse than being a plaintiff in a lawsuit is being a defendant. A plaintiff at least has the choice of filing the suit or not, and can choose, to some extent, when and where the suit is filed and what issues are involved. A defendant has none of these choices. In a suit brought on meritorious grounds, a plaintiff has some justifiable hope of winning the suit, collecting an award of damages and, possibly, an award of the attorneys' fees and costs he or she has incurred in pursuing the suit.

The best many defendants can hope for is to have the court rule in their favor, in which case they pay their own often enormous legal fees and go home, although since 1994, courts may in their discretion award attorney fees and costs to a prevailing defendant in copyright infringement suits. At worst, a defendant is held to have transgressed the rights of the plaintiff, is ordered to pay the plaintiff money damages, is enjoined from further conduct of the sort the plaintiff sought to have stopped, and has to pay the plaintiff's legal fees in addition to his or her own lawyers' fees. Sometimes plaintiffs come out ahead in lawsuits; defendants almost never do, even if the judgment is in their favor.

Theory Versus Practice

Our judicial system is, in theory, one of the best ever invented. In practice, it often leaves a great deal to be desired. Some disputes cannot be settled out of court and must be litigated to avoid injustice, but too often litigation is commenced because someone is trying to prove a point or hold a grudge or gets greedy. Copyright infringement suits in particular can make even the lawyers involved tired. This is because the issues involved in any copyright infringement suit are usually highly technical and because the egos of the parties to the suit may be more involved in the litigation than in, say, a suit where one insurance company is suing another.

In evaluating any potential lawsuit, remember that while it is important to be right, what you really want is to be right *out* of court. That means careful choices in your business relationships, careful attention to the rights of others, and a careful lawyer who counsels you on ways to avoid disputes before they ripen into lawsuits.

CHAPTER 7

Copyright in the Marketplace

NOBODY CAN TELL you what your copyright is worth. You may create a photograph today that you allow someone to use to illustrate a magazine article in return for payment of a few hundred dollars only to find that, years from now, your photograph is worth thousands, as a piece of art or because of its subject matter, or because of the growth of your fame as a photographer. And this invisible thing called a copyright can be subdivided and sold to as many people as you choose for long or short periods and you can, in the end, still own it after profiting from these exploitations of it. An author who understands the infinitely divisible nature of copyright can more easily profit from his or her work by paring off and selling, one at a time, the rights to use the work. If you can conceive of a division of copyright and convince someone to acquire the portion of your copyright that you offer for sale, you can turn your creation into money in your pocket.

Exploiting Copyrights

The "exploitation" of copyrights is like the cultivation of a garden. Although a copyrighted work may become very valuable, its earning power is only speculative until someone sells it, or the right to use it. Some authors exploit their own copyrights; this is typical of graphic designers and freelance writers. Some depend on others to turn their copyrighted works into cash flow; for example, songwriters and book authors depend on music and book publishers to create income for them. Sometimes authors and artists are lucky enough to find professionals who will help them sell their works. This is what literary agents, artists' reps, and gallery owners do, for a share of any proceeds. If you depend on the services of someone else to help you exploit your copyrights—and especially if you exploit your own copyrights—you need a thorough understanding of the three ways copyright rights are owned and change hands. If you are someone who acquires copyrights for exploitation, good business practice dictates that you acquire ownership rights that are valid, since enforceable ownership is a prerequisite to any exploitation of a copyright. The three ways that copyright ownership is transferred are: work-for-hire, assignment of copyright, and license of copyright.

Works Made for Hire

In ordinary circumstances, the author of any work eligible for copyright protection owns the copyright in that work from the creation of the work. This is not true when an employee creates a work as a part of his or her job; in that case, the work is a "work made for hire," which means that the employer is considered both the copyright owner and the author of the work from the inception of the work. Any full-time employee of a newspaper who writes a news story has created that story as a work made for hire. The same is true of a graphic artist who creates an illustration for a client of the advertising agency that employs him or a staff composer who writes the soundtrack for an industrial training film produced by the production company she works for.

Works created on or after January 1, 1978 by freelance creatives cannot be works made for hire unless certain requirements are met. There must be a written document in which both the creator of the work and the person commissioning it agree that it is to be considered a work made for hire *and* it must fall into one of the nine classes of works enumerated in the copyright statute as kinds of works that may be works made for hire if specially ordered or commissioned from an independent contractor, that is, a freelancer who is not a regular employee of the commissioning party.

The present copyright statute endeavors through the use of very specific language to clarify the confusion that formerly surrounded works made for hire. However, although the new, improved statutory language has helped matters, it has not entirely eliminated the confusion—and misunderstandings and lawsuits—that sometimes arise over the question of ownership of copyright in works created by one person at the behest of another. Because this is such an important issue, a detailed discussion of the circumstances that result in the work made for hire status is appropriate.

The threshold determination that must be made in deciding whether a work is or can be a work made for hire is whether the creator of the work is an employee or an independent contractor. This determination is often not as simple as it would seem. Of course, anyone who shows up five days a week at the same workplace, is issued regular paychecks, and receives a W-2 form every January from the company that issues those paychecks is an employee of that company. Any work created by that employee *within the scope of his or her duties as an employee* is a work made for hire. For instance, it is clear that a man who is employed full-time as a computer software designer owns the copyright in the novel he writes in his spare time. Unfortunately, it is not always so clear whether a worker is an employee.

Who Is an Employee?

In the first important decision interpreting the present copyright statute's work-for-hire provisions, the Supreme Court held that in deciding whether an author is an employee, it is appropriate to consider whether the party who commissioned the work in question has the right to control the manner and means by which the work is produced. Several factors were said to be relevant to this evaluation. These factors are:

- the skill required to produce the work;
- the source of the instrumentalities and tools that will be used to produce the work;
- on whose premises the work will be produced;
- the duration of the relationship between the party who commissions the work and the person who will create it;
- whether the party who commissions the work has the right to assign additional projects to the person who will create the work;
- the extent of the discretion that may be exercised by the person who will create the work over when and how long he or she works during the process of creating it;
- the method by which the person who creates the work will paid for his or her services;
- the role of the party who commissions the work in hiring and paying assistants for the person who will create the work;
- whether the work is part of the regular business of the party who commissions it;
- whether the party who commissions the work is in business;
- whether the party who commissions the work provides employee benefits to the person who will create the work; and
- the tax treatment of the person who will create the work.

None of these factors is, by itself, determinative. However, generally speaking, the more control the commissioning party has over the duties, work hours, and workplace of the person who creates a copyrightable work, the more likely that person is an employee. If you find yourself working for someone in a situation where your status, i.e., whether you are an employee, is indeterminate, don't guess who owns the copyrights in the products of your labor. Seek advice from a lawyer to clarify the nature of your arrangement if any part of your work involves the creation of anything that is copyrightable.

Assuming that a worker does not qualify as an employee of a party who commissions the creation of a copyrightable work, that worker is what the law calls an "independent contractor"; many independent contractors who work in the arts call themselves "freelancers." Any writer, artist, composer, or other author who works for many clients in his or her own office or studio (etc.), is paid only on a fee basis, and receives 1099 forms in January from those who pay for his or her services, is probably a freelancer. That being the case, the question then becomes *What works created by a freelancer are or may be works made for hire?*

Which Works May Be Works Made for Hire?

The copyright statute is specific in naming the sorts of works that may be agreed to be works made for hire. The statute says that a work created by an independent contractor may be a work made for hire if it

> is specially ordered or commissioned for use as a contribution to a collective work, as a part of a motion picture or other audiovisual work, as a translation, as a supplementary work, as a compilation, as an instructional text, as a test, as answer material for a test, or as an atlas, if the parties expressly agree in a written instrument signed by them that the work shall be considered a work made for hire. For the purpose of the foregoing sentence, a "supplementary work" is a work prepared for publication as a secondary adjunct to a work by another author for the purpose of introducing, concluding, illustrating, explaining, revising, commenting upon, or assisting in the use of the other work, such as forewords, afterwords, pictorial illustrations, maps, charts, tables, editorial notes, musical arrangements, answer material for tests, bibliographies, appendixes, and indexes, and an "instructional text" is a literary, pictorial or graphic work prepared for publication and with the purpose of use in systematic instructional activities.

The meaning of this statutory language is easier to grasp with concrete examples of the sorts of works that are deemed to be appropriate works made for hire. Examples of the statute's enumerated categories of works are: a work commissioned for use as a contribution to a collective work (such as an article prepared specifically to be included in an encyclopedia); as a part of a motion picture or other audiovisual work (such as a musical composition written to be used as the soundtrack for a television spot or a slideshow presentation); as a translation (such as the English translation of the works of the French poet Jean Nicholas Arthur Rimbaud); as a supplementary work (such as a chart or graph used to illustrate a chapter in a book); as a compilation (such as research results compiled from several surveys for publication as a reference book); as an instructional text (such as a pamphlet instructing the consumer in the proper method for assembling a bicycle or other product); as a test (such as the standardized tests given school-children to gauge their progress): as answer material for a test (the correct answers to a test, to be used in grading individual students on their responses); or as an atlas (such as a road atlas of the United States) may be a work made for hire even if it is prepared by a freelancer.

Many freelancers object to work-for-hire agreements. They feel that, in most circumstances, work-for-hire agreements are unfair to freelance creative people. This problem stems in part from lack of information; quite often, the person commissioning a work from a freelancer does not realize that it is not necessary to acquire the work as a work made for hire in order to secure the right to use the work as planned. There are other ways to acquire the right to use a copyrighted work.

Assignments of Copyright

An "assignment" of copyright is like a sale of the copyright; the author and original copyright owner sells all or some of his or her exclusive rights of copyright for the entire term of copyright or a shorter period. Copyright assignments are also called "transfers" of copyright. Anyone who acquires any right of copyright by assign-ment can, in turn, sell that right to someone else.

An assignment of copyright makes a commissioning party the owner of the copyright in a work in just about the same way that a work for hire agreement does. The major pertinent difference is that with an assignment the freelancer can elect to terminate the transfer of copyright rights between the thirty-fifth and thirty-sixth year of the term of copyright; under a work for hire agreement, the commis-sioning party is considered the "author" of the work from its creation and owns the copyright for the full term of copyright (seventy-five years from creation), with no possibility that the freelancer can terminate that term midway.

In the case of many works, thirty-five years is as good as forever. For these works, acquiring an assignment of the copyright in the work is sufficient to protect the interests of the commissioning party.

However, an assignment, or sale, of copyright does not have to be for the full term of copyright. Perfectly valid assignments can be made for one year or three years or twenty-five years—in short, for as long as you wish, up to and including the full term of copyright. This fact gives a freelancer the option of agreeing that the copyright in a work belongs to the commissioning party for the full period of time that the commissioning party believes it will want to use the work or needs to restrict any such use by any other party with whom the freelancer might otherwise contract. At the end of that period, all rights in the creative work automatically revert to the freelancer.

Often freelancers object to transferring ownership of their copyrights to those who will use them almost as much as they object to work-for-hire agreements. This is because many commissioning parties routinely ask for an assignment of all the exclusive rights of copyright for the full term of copyright. This leaves the author of the work with no further control over use of the work for the period of time the transfer is effective. In cases like this, the best solution is a license of copyright tailored to the client's needs. Unfortunately, clients are sometimes greedy. For example, clients often do not distinguish between payment for the services of a freelancer and payment for the right to use the copyrighted work the freelancer's services produce. Their attitude can be *What do you mean I've only paid for your work writing this article? For* that *amount of money, I want to own it.*

Freelancers also must be wary of clients who try to extort copyright ownership from them by trying to make payment for their services conditional on the transfer of the copyright in the work produced. It is not unheard of for a commissioning party to insert language on the back of the check sent in payment for a freelancer's services that purports to transfer "all rights" to the commissioning party when the freelancer endorses the check for deposit. Since the terms of an agreement must be actually consented to by both parties to the agreement before there is a legally binding contract, and because legitimate transfers of copyright typically mention "all rights of copyright" specifically and at length in very unambiguous language, the effect of such trickery is dubious. However, if you have signed such a document, the only way to prove that you did not mean to assign the copyright in your work to the person who paid to have it produced may be in the course of a lawsuit, which is a tedious and expensive way to prove anything.

Never sign any document unless you understand it completely. And mark out any language that seems out of place on a check in payment for work for a client, writing your initials in the margin beside the deleted language; this probably won't have any effect on whether the check will be honored by the client's bank, but it may keep you out of a lawsuit to prove that you still own the copyright in the work you produced.

Licenses of Copyright

A "license" to use a copyrighted work is like a lease of the intangible copyright or of part of it; a copyright owner can grant as many licenses, or permissions, to use the copyright, as he or she wants. These licenses may overlap or may divide the rights of copyright among several people. The copyright owner maintains ownership of the copyright, because, although he or she has agreed to allow the work to be used by someone else, no transfer of ownership of the copyright is made. *Non-exclusive* licenses are permissions to use a work in a specified way that may be granted to more than one user. *Exclusive* licenses grant to only one licensee at a time the right to use a work in a specified way.

Non-Exclusive Licenses

If a freelancer does not sign any written agreement regarding a work he or she creates, even if it is specially commissioned, the only right conveyed by the freelancer's action in delivering the work to the commissioning party is the right to use that work under a non-exclusive license. That is, the freelancer is under no obligation to refrain from granting a similar license or even selling the copyright in the work to someone else.

Non-exclusive licenses are also created when a copyright owner permits another person or company to use a work for a stated period of time, for specified purposes, and within a stated area but does not agree to avoid permitting the same or overlapping uses by others who request and pay for similar non-exclusive licenses in the work. For example, a photographer could agree to give an advertising agency the right to use her landscape photograph within the United States for ads for a client during a period of five years but could reserve the right to also license the photo to others, such as a travel magazine or a publisher of nature posters. In most non-exclusive licenses, no specific "reservation-of-rights" language is used; rather, the license merely provides that the licensee may make a certain use of the copyrighted work but does *not* state that the license is granted solely to that licensee.

The law does not require a non-exclusive license to be in writing. However, a verbal non-exclusive license is terminable at will by the copyright owner.

Exclusive Licenses

In the case of an *exclusive* license, the copyright owner grants to another person the sole right (that is, that person is the *only* person who has the right) to exercise some or all of her or his exclusive rights of copyright for a specified time. Again, this right may be exercised for as long or as short a period of time, for all or only certain specified purposes, and everywhere or within only a stated geographic area, depending on the terms of the license. For example, a photographer could agree to give an advertising agency the exclusive right to use his landscape photograph within the United States for ads for a client corporation during a period of five years but could reserve the right to sell the photo in Europe (to a magazine, perhaps) during that five-year period and to anyone anywhere for any use thereafter.

While assignments of copyright usually give the person or company to whom the assignment is made (called the "assignee") the right to use a freelancer's creative work in any way the assignee sees fit during the period of assignment, exclusive licenses usually specify a more limited scope of permitted use. For example, a painter could grant to a publisher the exclusive right to prepare and sell within the United States prints of one of her paintings; other publishers could be granted similar rights in other countries, and other people entirely could be given the right to reproduce the painting on tin cookie containers or calendars.

Like assignments, copyright licenses can ordinarily also be sold to someone else unless the written license prohibits such a sale. Any time a copyright owner assigns or licenses to someone else an exclusive right of copyright there must be a written agreement to that effect, signed by the copyright owner.

Benefits of Recordation

Any written assignment or exclusive license agreement may be recorded in the Copyright Office in order to document that the particular right(s) transferred or licensed exclusively are owned by someone other than the person who created the copyrighted work; recording an assignment or license is a very good idea in the case of any creative work of more than temporary significance.

Recording an assignment or exclusive license of copyright confers several benefits that are similar to those real property owners enjoy when they record deeds to land and buildings. However, since a copyright is intangible and because rights in copyright can be transferred merely by signing a document, recording the documents that transfer ownership of all or part of it is, perhaps, even more important than with real property.

The first and maybe the most important benefit of recording a copyright transfer or license is that such recordation creates a public record of ownership of the copyright or part of it. This can be very important in the case of a dishonest or completely uninformed author. If an author or other copyright owner transfers ownership of a copyright to one person and subsequently signs documents that purport to transfer the same copyright to another person, the recordation of the first transfer document by the first buyer will establish that buyer's priority with regard to ownership of the copyright. More than a few lawsuits have arisen from just such situations.

Secondly, recording assignments or exclusive licenses of copyright creates a public record of ownership of the subject copyrights.

This creates the records necessary to allow someone searching for the owner of a copyright to find the *current* owner, and allows those who are considering buying copyrights to search Copyright Office records to verify ownership of the copyrights.

The Copyright Office will record just about any document pertaining to a copyright that you feel should be recorded. In addition to the written assignment or exclusive license document, *signed by the person making the assignment or license,* you must fill out and send a Document Cover Sheet, with the proper fee to the Documents Unit, Cataloging Division of the Library of Congress. You can order blank Document Cover Sheets by calling the Copyright Office Forms Hotline at (202) 707-9100.

Choice of Method

Now that you understand the differences between copyright licenses and assignments and work-for-hire agreements, you can gauge which is appropriate and fair in a given situation. It's simply a matter of considering the rights conveyed by each in light of the practical aspects of the situation.

In the case of a specially commissioned work, an assignment is like a sales contract by which a freelancer transfers all copyright rights in a creative work to a commissioning party; in the assignment, the freelancer can negotiate a "sales figure" that adequately compensates him or her for his or her services in creating the work and for the sale of the copyright for the period of time agreed upon. If the assignment transfers rights in an existing work, that is, a work not specially commissioned, the freelancer's compensation may be less.

With an exclusive license, the freelancer also negotiates both the duration of the license (which is like a lease period) and a fair price for giving up the rights of copyright for that time period, but further bases his or her price on the scope of the exclusive license; that is, he or she considers the rights retained as well as those bargained away. Copyright owners who grant non-exclusive licenses consider the same factors, but the prices they can command will probably be much smaller than for an exclusive license, since the copyright owner who grants an non-exclusive license doesn't give up the right to grant the same permission to use the work—to one or a hundred other people.

It is to the advantage of an assignee or licensee to include language in an assignment or license agreement that allows the editing or other modification of the work to accommodate its intended use. It is to the author's advantage that the assignment or license agreement include language that provides for a re-use fee whenever the work is used.

A work-for-hire agreement, which really should be used only in situations that fit the copyright statute's requirements for works for hire, is the most exhaustive way of vesting rights in a commissioning party. This is because in a work-for-hire agreement a freelancer forfeits not only any ownership of the copyright in the work but also any right to further payment for any use of the work. He or she has no say as to how the work is used and cannot even demand credit if the work is displayed or published. Fair-minded business people will demand work-for-hire agreements only when they are really necessary and will be prepared to pay the freelancer enough to compensate him or her appropriately under all the circumstances of the situation.

In any business situation involving intangible properties like copyrights, it's smart for all parties to have a very good idea, in advance, of their respective rights and obligations. In the past, the law accommodated the assumption that any specially commissioned work was prepared as a work made for hire. This is not now the case and anyone whose business involves the creation or use of copyrights must adjust to this new reality and leave less to unvoiced assumptions.

In the this book's Appendix there are four form agreements for transferring interests in copyright. They are: an assignment; an exclusive license; a non-exclusive license; and a work-for-hire agreement. The language of the agreements is essentially the same except for the paragraphs which specify what rights are conveyed. If you read these agreements you should understand better how copyrights operate in the marketplace. You may also want to copy one or more of them for your own use.

Written Agreements

A contract is a set of legal rights and responsibilities created by the mutual agreement of two or more people or business entities—the "rules," so to speak, by which a particular business relationship is to be run. A contract is the agreement itself, not the paper document that memorializes the agreement. In fact, many contracts don't even have to be in writing to be valid, although, as we shall see, written contracts are almost always a good idea.

Except in old movies, written contracts do not depend for their effectiveness on complicated legal language. The goal of a good contract lawyer is to "draft," or write, a document that sets out in completely unambiguous language the agreement reached between the parties. This generally means that the more clearly a contract is written the more effective it is as a contract; but eliminating ambiguity may also require more detailed language than most people are accustomed to using and may result in a much longer written agreement than the contract lawyer's client thinks is necessary. However, in a skillfully drafted agreement *every* provision is necessary. Even in the case of an apparently simple agreement, a good contract lawyer will write an agreement that not only specifies what happens when the agreement is working but also what happens when it stops working.

The Structure of a Contract

There is no particular "architecture" required to make a written document a contract. What determines whether a document is a binding agreement is the content of the language, not the form in which the language is arranged in the document. Yet, there are certain standard sections into which formal written agreements are customarily divided.

The introductory section of a formal written agreement gives the names, and sometimes the addresses, of the parties to the agreement, indicates their legal status (an individual doing business under a trade name, a partnership, or a corporation), gives the short terms by which the contracting parties will be referred to in the agreement ("Megan Clark Bowers, hereinafter referred to as the

'Writer' . . ."), and specifies the date the agreement is made or is agreed to become effective.

The "premises" section of a formal written agreement sets out, sometimes after the word "Whereas," the set of circumstances upon which the agreement is founded, or "premised." This section makes certain representations about the facts that have influenced the parties' decision to enter the agreement and, although it may look like excess language to non-lawyers, in reality it sets out information that could be important if, in a lawsuit based on the agreement, a court had to "construe," or interpret, the written agreement in order to rule on the intent of the parties when they entered the agreement.

In the body of the written agreement, most contracts enumerate the various points of agreement between the parties in a series of headlined paragraphs, each of which sets out one facet of the agreement and all of which probably use the word "shall" to indicate the mandatory nature of the action expected from each party.

Besides all the major points of the agreement, a formal contract will also contain what are sometimes entitled "miscellaneous provisions" and what lawyers often call "boilerplate." These provisions look unnecessary to most non-lawyers, since, among other things, they set out methods for handling various contingencies that may never occur, but they can be crucially important. For example, one standard miscellaneous provision provides that any lawsuit based on the agreement will be filed in the courts of a specified state or city and that any dispute will be decided according to the laws of a specified state. This sort of provision can determine whether you sue to enforce your agreement in your home state or, at increased expense, in a distant city.

The Benefits of Written Agreements

No lawyer can include any provision in any written agreement that will compel ethical conduct from a dishonest person. The best any lawyer can do is include provisions in the written agreement that prescribe penalties for failure to abide by the terms of the contract, and even this will not ensure that a dishonest person does not act dishonestly. Your best protection against truly dishonest people is to avoid entering agreements with them, since a true renegade has little fear of lawsuits. In any event, having to go to court to obtain what, by rights, you were due under the terms of the agreement you made is an expensive, time-consuming, and frustrating experience.

Many business people, especially those who work in the creative fields, assume that written contracts between people who know and trust each other are unnecessary and that having lawyers prepare a written agreement in such a case is an avoidable expense. Neither of these assumptions is true. Even if you enter a business agreement with another ethical person, a written agreement is necessary for precision and for documentation.

Even honest and knowledgeable people sometimes fail to communicate to each other all the terms of their agreement. Putting an agreement in writing lets both parties "see" their agreement and provides an opportunity for them to negotiate points of the agreement they have previously omitted from their discussions. Further, a written agreement serves to document the terms of the arrangement throughout the life of the business arrangement. Human memory is fallible; even honest people can forget the precise terms of their agreements if they are not written down. And a written agreement can be crucial to proving the existence of the agreement if one of the people who originally made the agreement leaves his or her job for another company or, in the case of an individual, dies.

Generally, the more complex the terms of the agreement and the longer its duration, the more it should be documented in writing. Further, while it may be desirable and good business practice to reduce most agreements to writing, some sorts of agreements are not valid or enforceable unless they are in writing. For example, the United States copyright statute requires assignments and exclusive licenses of copyrights to be in writing and provides that no creation of an independent contractor can be a work made for hire unless there is a written agreement to that effect. And contracts which may not be performed within a year are required, almost everywhere, to be in writing.

All these are good reasons for consulting a lawyer when you enter an agreement of any importance. A good contract lawyer who is familiar with your business and your concerns can not only help you define and document your agreement, but can advise you concerning the law that governs your business relationship and suggest contract provisions that can help you reach your goals and avoid disputes.

Negotiating Contracts

Consulting a lawyer can be just as important, or even more important, when the written contract was drafted by lawyers for the other party. In any business agreement it is important to remember that there are actually two sorts of possible written contracts documenting the relationship—their version and your version.

This is especially true when the contracting parties are not equal in power, such as when a freelancer is presented with an agreement drafted by a publishing company. Having a lawyer on your side in a situation like this can help you feel less like David confronting Goliath. Your lawyer can explain complex contract provisions to you and, by negotiating on your behalf, turn the offered agreement into one that allows you more control, gets you paid more quickly, and is generally more favorable than the un-negotiated contract you were offered originally.

However, your lawyer must know something about your business before he or she can do an effective job for you. If you take a work-for-hire agreement to your friend the real estate lawyer and he says "Great! I've always wondered what one of these things looked like," it's time to consult another lawyer.

Nobody ever fights over an unsuccessful project. The more successful your book or song or poster, the more important it is to have the agreements concerning it reduced to unambiguous writing. This is true in most areas of business, but it is especially true with regard to any sort of intellectual property. Copyrights are intangible, but they are valuable, and their ownership and the business arrangements surrounding them should be in writing; on paper, in contracts.

Copyright in Cyberspace

Any analysis of copyright in the marketplace would be incomplete without a discussion of the newest and largest area of the copyright marketplace—the Internet. Lots of people seem to think that copyright can't survive in cyberspace. They think that existing copyright laws don't work in this new dimension for exploitation of copyrights and that inserting any work into the traffic on the information superhighway is tantamount to giving it away. Fortunately, these assumptions are untrue.

First, consider that the present copyright statute states that "copyright protection subsists . . . in original works of authorship fixed in any tangible medium of expression, now known or later developed, from which they can be perceived, reproduced, or otherwise communicated, either directly or with the aid of a machine or device." This language allows copyright to stretch when it is necessary to extend protection to new forms of expression without language that names each new technology. So, copyright has not been killed by the new methods of communications that are now possible via the Internet. In fact, it has expanded; the copyright umbrella is enlarged by virtue of the new forms of expression to which it now applies.

Secondly, copyright is not abandoned when a work is made accessible to millions via the Internet. Like the broadcast spectrum, cyberspace belongs to all of us. However, so do highways. Use of a public communications or transportation thoroughfare does not deprive you of your private property. Your car still belongs to you, no matter how many public roads you use. And the producers of television and radio programs still own the copyrights in the programs they broadcast over public airwaves. This is not to say that there is no danger of having your property stolen by "highwaymen" on the information superhighway, but, then, the risk of car theft exists on our roadways and people do make infringing copies of television and radio programs.

Proposed Cyberspace Copyright Legislation

In 1993 the White House formed the National Information Infrastructure (NII) Task Force to study the question of regulating the new frontier of cyberspace. The NII's Working Group on Intellectual Property Rights issued a study sometime later that assesses the question of copyright protection in cyberspace, among other issues.

Basically, the Working Group decided that the existing copyright statute is sufficient, with a few small changes, to protect copyright owners whose works are accessible to the public via the Internet.

The recommendations of the Working Group have now been codified into a proposed new law, the NII Copyright Protection Act. There are four basic parts to the proposed law. The proposed statute would:

- clarify current copyright law by emphasizing that copyright owners have the exclusive right to distribute copies of their works by transmitting them over computer networks even though no physical objects embodying the works change hands;
- broaden existing exceptions to copyright protection by allowing, without the permission of copyright owners, some digital copying of works by libraries and for the use of blind people;
- outlaw any device or service that can break encryption codes or in any way circumvent other efforts of copyright owners to protect their works from unauthorized copying; and
- forbid any tampering with or falsification of any digital tags or other means of identifying the owners of copyrighted works.

Almost any sort of work is susceptible to copying via the Internet. A coalition of copyright owners and users who appeared during hearings on the proposed NII Copyright Protection Act before the Senate Judiciary Committee early in 1996 demonstrated the ease with which works may be copied. The senators were shown how a movie, a book, a music video, and a secured test could be downloaded, sometimes at no cost, without the permission of the copyright holders or any compensation to them.

The proposed law would clear up many of the questions copyright owners have about the risks involved in allowing their works to be disseminated over the Internet. And copyright owners are already going after cyberspace pirates. Movie studios, performing rights societies, licensing agencies, software manufacturers, and trade associations have been surveying the materials available on the Internet with the intention of identifying and stopping pirates. Some lawsuits have been filed already. *Playboy* sued a network bulletin board for infringing its copyrights in its risqué photographs of attractive young women and won. The video game maker Sega sued and shut down a company that duplicated and sold its game software without its permission. Such efforts will in time create case law to define with great precision what is and is not Internet infringement. This will inform Internet users and most will abide by the law. Would-be pirates will be discouraged from trampling on the rights of copyright owners by news stories of large penalties levied against other pirates; after all, other, more familiar, communications technologies presently make unauthorized copying easy, but few crooks are willing to, say, press up a few hundred thousand copies of the latest Michael Bolton CD, because they know that Mr. Bolton's record company will come after them with whole platoons of copyright lawyers.

However, there is little likelihood that all danger of unauthorized copying will ever be eliminated. Copyright owners must, for example, take into consideration that few of us have the clout or the war chests of Paramount or BMI or Lotus. The best alternative to suing infringers, provided you can even discover where in cyberspace they are lurking, is to obviate the necessity for suing. That is, it is easier to keep the cat in the bag than to chase him down after he has been let out.

Assessing Electronic Publication

This means that any copyright owner should carefully consider the wisdom of making any work accessible via the Internet. As a practical matter, there is no guarantee that any work the habitués of the Internet can find in cyberspace won't be copied and distributed in ways the owner of copyright in the work objects to. Copyright notice and warnings forbidding unauthorized downloading and dissemination of a work are fine, but they stop only those scrupulous enough to refrain from infringing other people's copyrights. Lots of other Internet users, who are often young, brash, and enchanted with the (mistaken) idea that there is no law on the cyberspace frontier to restrict their actions, are not so conscientious. And encryption codes and devices are a great idea, but somebody will know how to get around most such barriers to infringement. After all, hackers can break into the computer systems of the government and big corporations; breaking the average encryption code can't be impossible.

There are several characteristics of a copyrighted work that may be determinative in any decision whether to launch the work into cyberspace. One is the popularity of the work and the desirability of disseminating it or owning a copy of it. You may post your fake-Hemingway short story on a bulletin board with perfect safety if it is so bad that no one wants to read it, much less copy it or claim authorship of it or send it electronically to all his or her friends. However, if your science fiction story is good and is interesting to enthusiasts of that genre, you may have a problem. Think about how likely it is that what you put into cyberspace will be stolen and/or further disseminated. Unless you are willing to, in effect, surrender your copyright rights in your work, think twice about putting into an "instant-infringement" form.

Consider, too, the nature of your work. Fact-based works, especially. Works that are primarily compilations of information and contain very little expression, such as directories, are granted much narrower copyright protection than creative works. This is the reason that publishers of large annual reference works that list, for instance, names and addresses of executives of corporations in a certain industry or the names and addresses of all the franchise restaurant companies in the United States, can be found only in the reference section of your local library. These publishers know that (a) the information in their directories is in demand; (b) their directories, because they are compilations of facts, are only narrowly protected by copyright law; and (c) they would be hard-pressed to stop infringers from lifting whole sections of the information they have gathered and published if their publications were accessible online. If you are doubtful about just how protectable your work is, don't make it easier for an infringer to steal it.

Electronic rights are a new area of law that grows and changes weekly. If you are offered any contract for the use of your work on the Internet, take it to a lawyer who is experienced in copyright law and get him or her to explain what you will be allowing by signing the agreement. The more important or potentially valuable your work, the more important it is that you look before you leap into an agreement that may give someone more rights in that work than you really want to give or allows it to be published in a form that makes unauthorized copying too easy.

No final statement can be made on any of the topics connected with copyrights in the cyberspace marketplace because cyberspace copyright is a cake that isn't baked yet. There are not yet enough reported court decisions to say exactly what the law is in every situation and, in any event, it seems likely that the statutes governing copyright in cyberspace will change—maybe more than once, in a sort of virtual evolution of this species of communications law. Until the cyberspace frontier has been settled, be cautious about what you insert into its commercial district. And stay tuned. The saga will continue.

CHAPTER 8

Recapture of Copyrights

I N 1976, THE UNITED STATES got a new copyright law, the first entirely new U.S. copyright law since 1909. Two provisions of the new copyright law, which became effective January 1, 1978, are of potentially great benefit to creative people, since they allow, under certain circumstances, the termination of previous transfers of copyright. (A "transfer" of copyright is an assignment or sale of copyright to someone else.) These provisions allow a creator of a work to make a sale of the copyright in the work and later cancel, or terminate, that sale and regain, or "recapture," ownership of the copyright. The "termination-of-transfers" provisions of the new law are somewhat complicated, but any author owes it to himself or herself—and his or her heirs—to learn a little about the new provisions and how they work.

There are two groups of copyrights that are affected by the new termination-of-transfers provisions. Section 203 of the new copyright law provides that an assignment of copyright made on or after January 1, 1978 by the author of a work may be terminated thirty-five to forty years after the assignment. Section 304(c) of the new copyright statute provides that assignments of copyright made by an author or certain members of the author's family before January 1, 1978 may be terminated after fifty-six years from the date copyright protection was first secured. The right to terminate an assignment is statutory; this means you can't waive this right or bargain it away.

When you (or certain of your heirs) exercise the right to terminate an assignment, on the date that the termination is effective you (or they) regain ownership of all the rights of copyright (with some limitations in specific situations) that were originally sold or otherwise conveyed to someone else. You (or your family) then own those rights for the remainder of the term of copyright (until fifty years after your death or the death of your last surviving co-author for works created on or after January 1, 1978, and for nineteen more years for works that have been protected by copyright for fifty-six years), or the copyright may be sold or licensed again. It's important to remember, however, that only U.S. copyright rights may be regained; the U.S. copyright law is only effective within the United States and its termination-of-transfers provisions affect only U.S. copyrights. Further, the termination-of-transfers provisions do not apply to copyrights that were created as works-for-hire.

The new copyright law sets out specific procedures that must be followed by anyone who seeks to terminate a transfer of copyright. Written notices of intent to terminate must be given, *by and to* the proper people, during specified periods in advance of termination. These notices will be ineffective to accomplish termination if they are given too soon or too late, or by or to the wrong people.

The termination of copyright transfers is a complicated area of the law that confuses even lawyers. This means that the termination of a copyright assignment is *not* a do-it-yourself job. If a copyright is valuable enough, decades after its creation, to make its ownership desirable, it's valuable enough to justify paying a copyright lawyer to help regain that ownership. However, before a lawyer can help you or your family regain ownership of a copyright, you or your heirs must first remember that such a procedure is possible and, second, you must be able to supply that lawyer with sufficient information about the original assignment of the copyright to enable him or her to carry out the termination. This means you should keep accurate records of every assignment of the copyright in any work you create. Keeping records concerning the assignments of your copyrights does not have to be time-consuming. The best way to keep the records you need is to set aside an evening once every year to compile records that could result in increased old-age income for you or enhanced income for your spouse, children, and grand-children after your death.

A form for recording important information about the copyrights in the works you create and assign to someone else appears at the end of this chapter. Make a supply of clear photocopies of the form, called "Notice to My Heirs and Executors." Fill out one of these forms for each assignment of copyright you make and attach to the filled-out form a copy of the work that was the subject of the assignment, a copy of the assignment document, and the copyright registration certificate, if you have one.

Put the records concerning all transfers of copyright made during any given year in a folder marked "Copyright Transfers—1997" (etc.). Keep these records with your other important personal papers; tell your spouse, your adult children, the executor of your will, and your lawyer you're keeping such records and why.

The termination-of-transfers provisions of the new copyright act were included in the statute because Congress wanted to give authors and their families the chance to regain ownership of copyrights that grow to be valuable after they are originally sold. In the case of terminations made after fifty-six years of copyright protection, Congress wanted to give authors the benefit of the nineteen-year extension period it tacked onto the end of the copy-right terms in existence when the new law was passed. The copy-right law is our government's way of rewarding and encouraging creativity in our society; the termination-of-transfers provisions of the new copyright law can help you make sure that your successful works benefit you and your heirs as well as others who exploit them.

FORM NOTICE TO MY HEIRS AND EXECUTORS

Follow the directions above for using this form to record information about assignments of copyrights so that those assignments of copyright may be later terminated, as provided in the U.S. copyright statute.

Notice to My Heirs and Executors

If the procedures specified in Sections 203 and 304(c) of the U.S. Copyright Act of 1976 are followed and certain requirements are met, the ownership of the copyright in the Work described below (referred to herein as "the Work") may be regained, by me or by my spouse, children, or grandchildren, even though I have previously assigned all or some part of the copyright in the Work to another person or company (referred to herein as "the Assignee"), as described below.

If the date of assignment listed below is before January 1, 1978, it is possible that the assignment may be terminated fifty-six years after copyright protection was secured.

If the date of assignment listed below is after January 1, 1978, it is possible that the assignment may be terminated between thirty-five and forty years after it was made.

The copyright in the Work may be very valuable. If the termination of the assignment of this copyright is not carried out correctly, the right to regain ownership of the copyright may be lost. This notice and any attachments[1] should be taken to a copyright lawyer not more than ten years and not less than three years (a) before the fifty-sixth anniversary of an assignment made prior to January 1, 1978, or (b) before the thirty-fifth anniversary of an assignment made after January 1, 1978.

A. Description of Work:[2]

_____

_____

_____

_____

_____

B. Author(s) of Work (indicate ownership share of the copyright for each author):[3]

_____

_____

_____

_____

_____

C. Date of Transfer of Copyright by Me:[4] _____

D. Percentage of Entire Copyright Transferred by Me:[5]_____

E. Copyright Assigned to: (indicate name of the Assignee, including the most current address and phone number available for the Assignee)[6]

_____

_____

_____

_____

_____

FORM NOTICE TO MY HEIRS AND EXECUTORS: NOTES

1. If it is possible to attach a copy of the Work that was the subject of the assignment, do so. This may be a photocopy of a work on paper, a photograph for a three-dimensional work, a diskette for a computer program, or a videocassette for an audiovisual work. Insert the copy of the Work in a large manila envelope that is durably attached to this form; enclose a copy of the document in which the copyright assignment was made, if it is available, and the original copyright registration certificate, if the copyright in the Work has been registered.

2. Start with an appropriate short description of the Work that was the subject of the assignment, i.e., "a photograph of three-year-old twin girls, each holding a black Labrador puppy," "a poem titled _Midsummer's Eve_," "a musical composition titled _Wind Dance_," "a short story titled 'High Hopes,'" "a non-fiction book manuscript titled _Butterflies of the Eastern States_," etc. Follow with a description of the Work detailed enough to allow anyone who may have a role in terminating the previous assignment to determine just which particular work, out of all similar works, was the subject of the assignment.

If it is practicable, attach a copy of the Work, similar to the sort of copies required for registration of copyright, to each original of the Assignment of

Copyright document. If it is not practicable to do so, omit this language and use a much more detailed description of the Work or use photographs (for three-dimensional works such as sculptures) or other identifying material, such as the script for a film, and change the language describing the attached materials.

3. Insert the names of all the authors here. For example, if you and a co-author created the Work together, use language similar to the following: "Megan Bowers, fifty percent (50%) author of the Work and Natalie Wilson, fifty percent (50%) author of the Work." If you created the Work alone, make that fact clear by using language similar to the following: "Aaron Bowers, sole author of the entire Work."

4. Insert the date of the assignment of copyright in the Work, i.e., the date of the publishing agreement or other document that transferred ownership of the copyright in the Work to someone else.

5. In the usual circumstance, you will assign your entire interest in the copyright in the Work and will use language here similar to the following: "one hundred percent (100%)" If you created the Work with a co-author and assigned only your portion of the copyright, use language similar to the following: "fifty percent (50%) of the entire copyright in the Work." Make sure you use language that jibes with the information you gave in Paragraph B. That is, if you originally owned one-half of the copyright in the Work and assigned to a publishing company only half of your one-half ownership share, you would use "twenty-five percent (25%) of the entire copyright in the Work," since half of a one-half share of a whole is one-quarter, or twenty-five percent.

6. Insert the name, address, and phone number of the Assignee named in the document that assigned ownership of the copyright in the Work to someone else.

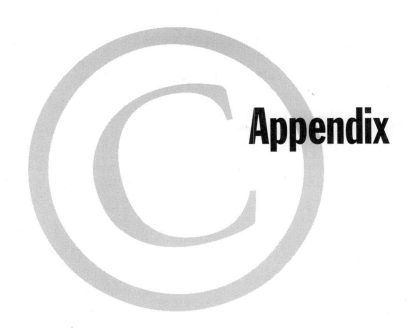

Appendix

FORM PERMISSION REQUEST LETTER

Because copyright law does not require non-exclusive licenses of copyright and because most permissions to use copyrighted works fall into this category, most permissions don't need to be in writing. However, a written permission is an excellent idea, if for no other reason than that the person requesting the permission and the one granting it will have, in writing, documentation of the scope of the permission. This form permission request letter allows the would-be user of a work to request and receive permission to use the work in one document. Use a version of this form letter to request permission to use any work that is not a public domain work.

Timothy Wilson St. Charles[1]
726 Edgemont Avenue
Montclair, New Jersey 94202
January 30, 1997

Ms. Lulu Bluestocking[2]
630 Park Avenue
New York, NY 10021

Dear Ms. Bluestocking,[3]

I am researching the life of your late friend Marshall Litterateur in preparation for writing a critical biography of Mr. Litterateur.[4] Magellan Press of Nashville, a noted publisher of scholarly non-fiction, has contracted to publish my book.[5]

In this connection, I am writing to request your permission to quote from your letters to Mr. Litterateur between the years 1949 and 1951.[6] Your kind donation of these letters to the Harry Ransom Humanities Research Center at the University of Texas in Austin has made it possible for me to gain a more complete picture of Mr. Litterateur's life and writings during those years.[7]

I have attached to this letter a list of the excerpts from your letters that I would like to quote in my manuscript.[8] You will note that in any instance where you mentioned a person who is still living, I have referred to that person in the excerpt I have made as "Miss A" or "Mr. B" in order to preserve her or his privacy, as well as yours.[9] Similarly, you will note that I have not included in the excerpts I am requesting permission to publish any material that is not of legitimate interest to literary scholars; specifically, in three of the excerpts that appear on the third page of the attachment I have omitted several passages of a purely personal nature that could possibly embarrass your son or Mr. Litterateur's grandchildren.[10]

I also enclose photocopies of several photographs, also from the collections of the Harry Ransom Center. I believe that the first four of these photographs were taken by you at your country house in Connecticut during the six years that Mr. Litterateur spent his summers with you there. I want to include these photos in my book. I need your permission to reproduce them.[11] I also need your consent to the publication of the two photos of you with Mr. Litterateur, one in your parlor at Stonehaven and one on the front porch there, photocopies of which are also enclosed.[12] These photographs were taken by your and Mr. Litterateur's mutual friend Clare Bratten, who, as owner of the copyrights in those photographs, has given me permission to publish them in my book.[13]

I enclose a letter from my publisher confirming my book contract and attesting to my reliability and competence as a biographer. Perhaps you have seen my previous book, a biography titled *Bon Mots: the Life and Works of Carolyn T. Wilson.*[14]

If you will consent to my request to reprint from your letters to Mr. Litterateur the excerpts listed on the attachment to this letter and the publication of the photos described above and enclosed in the form of photocopies, please countersign this letter in the space below reserved for your signature and return one copy of the letter and excerpts list to me in the enclosed, self-addressed, stamped envelope.[15] I am sending two copies of this letter and its attachment so that you may retain a copy for your files.[16]

Thank you for considering my request.

Sincerely,

Will St. Charles[17]

Agreed and accepted:

Lulu Bluestocking

_____ [18]   _____
SIGNATURE   DATE OF SIGNATURE

FORM PERMISSION REQUEST LETTER: NOTES

1. Insert your name and address here, or use stationery preprinted with your name and address.

2. Insert the name of the owner of the copyright in the work or works you want permission to use. This person may be the author of those works, as in this example, or may instead be the publisher or heir or executor of the estate of the author.

3. Insert the name of the person to whom the letter is addressed.

4. Briefly describe your project.

5. If you have a book contract or some other commitment that will result in the distribution and dissemination of your finished project, describe it here. If you have no such commitment, state your plans regarding your project, as "I intend to use excerpts from your letters in my dissertation; I am a Ph.D. candidate at the University of Wisconsin at Madison."

6. Describe as specifically as possible your source material. Further, if you can limit the scope of your request to include only material that you

may actually use, permission to use the material may be more easily obtained.

7. It's not a bad idea to state where and how you gained access to the materials you want to use, especially in the case of unpublished materials, as in this example, access to which may be restricted as a condition of the donor's gift of those materials to a library or other institution. However, if you have stumbled across useful material in a less conventional manner, such as discovering in a used-book store a cache of manuscripts with the author's notations concerning revisions, state the fact forthrightly. Deception of any sort is likely to make the person to whom you address your request suspicious of you and your motives.

8. Again, be as specific as possible about the material you want to use. The narrower the request, the more likely it is to be granted.

9. If it is possible to obscure the identity of living people who are mentioned in previously unpublished materials, such as the fictitious letters which are the subject of this permission letter, it may be desirable to do so. The owners of such materials may be reluctant to have their comments about identifiable living people published during their lifetime.

10. Similarly, the owners of copyright in unpublished materials may wish to avoid causing pain or embarrassment to their own or others' families by allowing the disclosure of their personal affairs; gaining permission to quote from unpublished materials may depend on your willingness and ability to shield the author of those materials and other concerned people.

11. The owner of the copyright in a photograph, under ordinary circumstances, is the photographer. Permission from the copyright owner is required to publish even snapshots of friends and relatives such as these. If a photograph depicts someone who is a public figure, such as the man who is the subject of the biography proposed in this form permission letter, it is not necessary to obtain permission from that person (or his or her heirs) for the use of that person's image in any non-commercial context.

12. However, in the situation portrayed in this form permission letter, the woman to whom the letter is addressed and who appears in two of the photos is a private individual who can and may object to the publication of photographs of herself. (For a more detailed discussion of the law of privacy and publicity, see the book by Lee Wilson, *Advertising: What's the Law*, forthcoming from Allworth Press.)

13. Again, it is necessary to obtain from the photographer permission to publish his or her photographs.

14. A letter such as this is not a job interview, but it doesn't hurt to briefly present your credentials to the person from whom you are requesting the permission; a track record and association with credible institutions can only bolster the chance that the requested permission will be granted.

15. Since this portion of the letter recites your proposed course of action and asks for the consent to that course of action from the person to whom the letter is addressed, it is very important to make sure that the language you use states exactly what you want permission to do. Any vague language may cast doubt on what was agreed to.

16. It is best to make it as easy as possible for the person from whom the permission is requested to say "yes" to your request. This means that you should not expect the person to whom you address your letter to have to photocopy it or type an envelope to return it to you.

17. Your signature on the letter will serve to demonstrate your agreement to abide by whatever conditions on the use of the materials you want to use that you have proposed to abide by.

18. Leave this space blank for the signature of the person who countersigns the letter. The signature of that person at the bottom of the letter transforms your proposal (to use and publish certain materials, on stated conditions) into an agreement between the two of you.

FORM ASSIGNMENT OF COPYRIGHT

To be legally effective, assignments of copyright must be in writing and must be signed by at least the owner of the copyright transferred; this form agreement is for use in transferring ownership of a copyright from the author of the work to another person or company.

Assignment of Copyright

This agreement is made between Megan Bowers[1] (hereinafter referred to as "the Author"[2]) and Ace Publishing Company[3] (hereinafter referred to as "the Assignee"), with reference to the following facts:

A. That the Author, an independent contractor,[4] is the creator of and owner of the copyright in a certain unpublished[5] drawing[6] (hereinafter referred to as "the Work"), which may be more fully described as follows:[7]

A three-by-five-inch pen-and-ink portrait of the poet Seamus Heaney, a photocopy[8] of which is attached hereto and made a part of this agreement by this reference.

B. That the Work was completed during 1996.[9]

C. That the Author's date of birth is July 7, 1951.[10]

The Author and the Assignee agree as follows:

1. That the Author hereby assigns, transfers, and conveys to the Assignee all[11] right, title, and interest in and to the Work described above[12] together with the copyright therein and the right to secure copyright registration therefor, in accordance with Sections 101, 204, and 205 of Title 17 of the United States Code, the Copyright Law of the United States. The above assignment, transfer, and conveyance includes, without limitation, any and all features, sections, and components of the Work, any and all works derived therefrom, the United States and worldwide copyrights therein, and any renewals or extensions thereof, and any and all other rights that the Author now has or to which he or she may become entitled under existing or subsequently enacted federal, state, or foreign laws, including, but not limited to, the following rights: to reproduce, publish, and display the Work publicly, to prepare derivative works of and from the Work, to combine the Work with other materials, and to otherwise exploit and control the use of the Work.[13] The above assignment further includes any and all causes of action for infringement of the Work, past, present, and future, and any and all proceeds from such causes accrued and unpaid and hereafter accruing; and

2. That the Assignee shall have the right to crop, edit, alter, or otherwise modify the Work to the extent that the Assignee, in the sole discretion of the Assignee, deems necessary to suit it to such uses as the Assignee may choose to make of the Work.[14]

3. That the Assignee will pay to the Author the sum of five hundred dollars ($500),[15] which amount it is agreed will constitute Author's only compensation for the grant of rights made herein.[16]

4. That the Author warrants that he or she is the owner of copyright in the Work and possesses full right and authority to convey the rights herein conveyed. The Author further warrants that the Work does not infringe the copyright in any other work, and does not invade any privacy, publicity, trademark, or other rights of any other person.[17] The Author further agrees to indemnify and hold the Assignee harmless in any litigation in which a third party challenges any of the warranties made by the Author in this

paragraph if any such litigation results in a judgment adverse to the Assignee in a court of competent jurisdiction;[18] and

5. That this agreement shall be governed by the laws of the State of Tennessee[19] applicable to contracts made and to be performed therein and shall be construed according to the Copyright Law of the United States, Title 17, Section 101, *et seq.,* United States Code; and

6. That this agreement shall inure to the benefit of and bind the parties and their respective heirs, representatives, successors, and assigns.[20]

In witness whereof, the Author and the Assignee have executed this document in two (2) counterpart originals[21] as of[22] the fifth day of September, 1996.[23]

_____ 24	_____ 25
AUTHOR	ASSIGNEE
_____ 26	_____ 27
ADDRESS	ADDRESS
_____	_____
_____	BY: _____ 28
SOCIAL SECURITY NUMBER[29]	
	_____
	TITLE[30]

FORM ASSIGNMENT OF COPYRIGHT: NOTES

1. Insert the name of the author of the work. If two or more people created the work as co-authors, insert all their names here and add enough spaces for their signatures, etc., at the end of the agreement.

2. If you want to be more specific, use "Photographer," "Writer," "Songwriter," "Composer," "Illustrator," etc.; use the same designation throughout the document everywhere the word "Author" appears here. If two or more people created the work as co-authors, use the following language: "(hereinafter jointly referred to as 'the Author')."

3. Insert the name of the person or company to whom the copyright in the work is being assigned, or transferred.

4. This form assignment agreement is inappropriate for use by anyone who is *not* an independent contractor. The works created by employees as

a part of their jobs are works-for-hire; no written agreement is necessary to document the work-for-hire situation in such a circumstance because the relationship of the employee and employer determines, as a matter of law, the ownership of the copyright in any work created on the job by the employee. However, even someone who works at a full-time job is an independent contractor with regard to any activity outside his or her job responsibilities. This language makes clear that the Author is not an employee of the Assignee. This is an important point because an author who does not create a work as part of his or her job responsibilities may terminate an assignment of the sort made in this agreement at the halfway point of copyright protection. (See chapter 4 for more information on terminations of copyright assignments.)

5. If the Work has been published, use language similar to the following to specify the year of first publication of the Work: "a certain drawing, first published in 1996." One of the three elements of copyright notice is the year date of first publication of the work. (See chapter 2 for more information about copyright notice.)

6. Use an appropriate short designation for the type of work that is the subject of the assignment, i.e., "a photograph of three-year-old twin girls, each holding a black Labrador puppy," "a poem titled *Midsummer's Eve*," "a musical composition titled *Wind Dance*," "a short story titled 'High Hopes,'" "a non-fiction book manuscript titled *Butterflies of the Eastern States*," etc.

7. Insert a detailed description of the Work sufficient to allow the parties to the assignment and everyone else to determine just which particular work, out of all similar works, is the subject of the assignment.

8. If it is practicable, attach a copy of the Work, similar to the sort of copies required for registration of copyright, to each original of the Assignment of Copyright document. If it is not practicable to do so, omit this language and use a much more detailed description of the Work or use photographs (for three-dimensional works such as sculptures) or other identifying material, such as the script for a film, and change the language describing the attached materials.

9. Specify the year during which the Work was finished by the Author. (This year date is required on any application for copyright registration.)

10. Insert the correct date. (The author's date of birth is also required on any application for copyright registration.)

11. It is, of course, possible to convey by assignment less than the entire

copyright in a work. If this is desired, use language similar to the following: "That the Author hereby assigns, transfers, and conveys to the Assignee fifty percent (50%) of the entire right, title, and interest in and to the Work described above . . .")

12. This assignment language does not convey ownership in any physical object or objects that embody the Work, since copyright ownership is separate from ownership of copies of the Work. If the parties intend to convey both the copyright in the work and ownership of a physical object or objects (such as a sculpture or an original painting), a separate sales agreement should be drafted to provide for the sale of any such physical object or objects. (However, as a practical matter, implied in any transfer of copyright in a work that requires possession of a particular physical object, such as a computer diskette (if the work in which copyright is transferred is computer software) to allow the work to be copied is the promise that the author of the work will at least make available for copying any such necessary physical object.

13. These are the exclusive rights of copyright given to copyright owners by the U.S. copyright statute and the copyright statutes of other countries.

14. Unless permission to alter the work is given by the Author of the work, anyone who significantly modifies it may be legally liable to the Author for distorting his or her work.

15. When they draft agreements, lawyers traditionally use both words and figures to specify sums of money one party must pay the other. This is done to diminish the possibility that a typographical error will lead to the underpayment of one party or overpayment by the other. It is a good rule to follow in modifying this form agreement for your own use.

16. If payment is to be made in installments, use language similar to the following: "That the Assignee will pay to the Author the sum of ten thousand dollars ($10,000), which amount it is agreed will constitute the Author's only compensation for the grant of rights made herein and which shall be paid according to the following schedule: five thousand dollars ($5,000) shall be paid upon the execution of this agreement; twenty-five hundred dollars ($2,500) shall be paid on a date not later than thirty days after the date of execution of this agreement; and twenty-five hundred dollars ($2,500) shall be paid on a date not later than sixty days after the date of execution of this agreement." The phrase "only compensation" refers to the fact that this agreement does not provide for the periodic payment of royalties to the Author, as do many agreements in which authors

transfer copyrights to others, such as book publishers or music publishers. This simple form Assignment of Copyright is inadequate to document a transfer of copyright made in return for the promise of the payment of royalties; while the *transfer* provisions of this assignment are adequate for such an arrangement, agreements that provide for the payment of royalties universally make many other provisions, such as a provision specifying the right of the author to occasionally examine the books of the assignee.

17. This sort of provision is common in assignments of copyright to protect the person or company acquiring the copyright from lawsuits for infringement based on actions of the Author. This seems reasonable if you consider that assignees usually have no knowledge of the circumstances surrounding the creation of the work of others and need to make sure that they are buying only copyrights, *not* lawsuits.

18. This is called a "hold harmless" clause and is very common in book publishing, music publishing, and other agreements in which one party acquires the copyright in a work created by an independent contractor. This is a fairly mild example of a hold harmless clause. Authors should expect to see provisions similar to those made in Paragraph 4 of this agreement in any document that transfers ownership of a copyright; no assignee should agree to buy a copyright unless the author of the work will make, in writing, promises similar to these in the document that transfers ownership of the copyright.

19. Insert the name of the state where you live here. It is an advantage to a litigant to be able to file or defend a suit in his or her home state. However, it may be that each party to the agreement will want any suit concerning it be filed in his or her home state. This is a point of negotiation but, as a practical matter, the more powerful of the two parties to the agreement will prevail.

20. This allows the Author to assign any sums due under the agreement to a third party or the estate of an Author who dies to collect any such sums on his or her behalf. It also permits the Assignee to in turn assign ownership of the copyright in the Work to another person or company. However, under some circumstances, especially those where the assignment is made in return for the periodic payment of royalties, the Author will not want the Assignee to assign the copyright in the Work to any other party; the usual reason for this objection is that the Author may not know and trust this secondary assignee and may have no confidence in the ability of any such secondary assignee to exploit the copyright in the Work. In such an event,

add this language to limit the right of the Assignee to assign the copyright to another entity: "However, the Assignee shall not attempt to convey any of the rights granted herein to the Assignee by the Author to any third party without the prior written consent of the Author."

21. Specify how many original copies of the agreement (i.e., copies of the agreement, even if they are photocopies) there are that bear the original signatures of the parties.

22. In agreements, "as of" means: "We are signing this agreement today, but we mean for it to take effect *as of* two weeks ago, or next month." A date specified that is before or after the agreement is actually signed is referred to as the "effective date" of the agreement.

23. If you want the agreement to become effective on the date it is signed, use that date here. If you want it to be effective as of a previous date, use that date. If you want to postpone the time when the agreement becomes operative until a later date, use that future date.

24. Leave this space blank for the signature of the Author.

25. Leave this space blank for the signature of the Assignee.

26. Insert the Author's address here.

27. Insert the Assignee's address here.

28. Insert here the name of a person who is acting on behalf of his or her company when that company is the Assignee. If the Assignee is an individual, this line may be omitted.

29. It may be necessary for the Assignee to file a report of the Assignee's payments to the Author with the Internal Revenue Service; if so, the Author's Social Security Number will be necessary for any such filings.

30. Insert here the title of a person who is acting on behalf of his or her company when that company is the Assignee. If the Assignee is an individual, this line may be omitted.

FORM EXCLUSIVE LICENSE OF COPYRIGHT

To be legally effective, exclusive licenses of copyright must be in writing and must be signed by at least the owner of the copyright licensed; this form agreement allows the author of a work to license it exclusively to another person or company.

Exclusive License of Copyright

This agreement is made between Natalie Wilson[1] (hereinafter referred to as "the Author"[2]) and Ace Publishing Company[3] (hereinafter referred to as "the Licensee"), with reference to the following facts:

A. That the Author, an independent contractor,[4] is the creator of and owner of the copyright in a certain unpublished[5] drawing[6] (hereinafter referred to as "the Work"), which may be more fully described as follows:[7]

A three-by-five-inch pen-and-ink portrait of the poet Seamus Heaney, a photocopy[8] of which is attached hereto and made a part of this agreement by this reference.

B. That the Work was completed during 1996.[9]

C. That the Author's date of birth is July 7, 1951.[10]

The Author and the Licensee agree as follows:

1. That the Author hereby grants to the Licensee the sole and exclusive right to reproduce, publish, prepare derivative works of and from, combine with other materials, display publicly, and otherwise use, control the use of, and exploit the Work[11] for a period of thirty-six (36)[12] months from the date written below.

2. That, during the term of this License of Copyright, the Licensee shall have the right to exercise the rights granted herein throughout the United States and Canada.[13]

3. That the Licensee shall have the right to crop, edit, alter, or otherwise modify the Work to the extent that the Licensee, in the sole discretion of the Licensee, deems necessary to suit it to such uses as the Licensee may choose to make of the Work.[14]

4. That the Licensee will pay to the Author the sum of five hundred dollars ($500), which amount it is agreed will constitute Author's only compensation for the grant of rights made herein.[15]

5. That the Author warrants that he or she is the owner of copyright in the Work and possesses full right and authority to convey the rights herein conveyed. The Author further warrants that the Work does not infringe the

copyright in any other work, and does not invade any privacy, publicity, trademark, or other rights of any other person.[16] The Author further agrees to indemnify and hold the Licensee harmless in any litigation in which a third party challenges any of the warranties made by the Author in this paragraph if any such litigation results in a judgment adverse to the Author in a court of competent jurisdiction;[17] and

6. That this agreement shall be governed by the laws of the State of Tennessee[18] applicable to contracts made and to be performed therein and shall be construed according to the Copyright Law of the United States, Title 17, Section 101, *et seq., United States Code;* and

7. That this agreement shall inure to the benefit of and bind the parties and their respective heirs, representatives, successors, and assigns.[19]

In witness whereof, the Author and the Licensee have executed this document in two (2) counterpart originals[20] as of[21] the fifth day of September, 1996.[22]

_____[23]
AUTHOR

_____[24]
LICENSEE

_____[25]
ADDRESS

_____[26]
ADDRESS

_____

_____

_____
SOCIAL SECURITY NUMBER[28]

BY: _____[27]

_____
TITLE[29]

FORM EXCLUSIVE LICENSE OF COPYRIGHT: NOTES

1. Insert the name of the author of the work. If two or more people created the work as co-authors, insert all their names here and add enough spaces for their signatures, etc., at the end of the agreement.

2. If you want to be more specific, use "Photographer," "Writer," "Songwriter," "Composer," "Illustrator," etc.; use the same designation throughout the document everywhere the word "Author" appears here. If two or more people created the work as co-authors, use the following language: "(hereinafter jointly referred to as 'the Author')."

3. Insert the name of the person or company to whom the copyright in the work is being licensed.

4. This form license agreement is inappropriate for use by anyone who is *not* an independent contractor. The works created by employees as a part of their jobs are works-for-hire; no written agreement is necessary to document the work-for-hire situation in such a circumstance because the relationship of the employee and employer determines, as a matter of law, the ownership of the copyright in any work created on the job by the employee. However, even someone who works at a full-time job is an independent contractor with regard to any activity outside his or her job responsibilities. This language makes clear that the Author is not an employee of the Licensee.

5. If the Work has been published, use language similar to the following to specify the year of first publication of the Work: "a certain drawing, first published in 1996." One of the three elements of copyright notice is the year date of first publication of the work. (See chapter 2 for more information about copyright notice.)

6. Use an appropriate short designation for the type of work that is the subject of the assignment, i.e., "a photograph of three-year-old twin girls, each holding a black Labrador puppy," "a poem titled *Midsummer's Eve*," "a musical composition titled *Wind Dance*," "a short story titled 'High Hopes,'" "a non-fiction book manuscript titled *Butterflies of the Eastern States*," etc.

7. Insert a detailed description of the Work sufficient to allow the parties to the license and everyone else to determine just which particular work, out of all similar works, is the subject of the license.

8. If it is practicable, attach a copy of the Work, similar to the sort of copies required for registration of copyright, to each original of the Exclusive License of Copyright document. If it is not practicable to do so, omit this language and use a much more detailed description of the Work or use photographs (for three-dimensional works such as sculptures) or other identifying material, such as the script for a film, and change the language describing the attached materials.

9. Specify the year during which the Work was finished by the Author. (The Copyright Office permits exclusive licensees to register with the Copyright Office their interests in the copyrights they license; the year date the Work was completed is required on any application for copyright registration.)

10. Insert the correct date. (The author's date of birth is also required on any application for copyright registration.)

11. These are the exclusive rights of copyright given to copyright owners by the U.S. copyright statute and the copyright statutes of other countries.

12. When they draft agreements, lawyers traditionally use both words and figures to specify important numbers and sums of money one party must pay the other. This is done to diminish the possibility that a typographical error will lead to a misunderstanding of some important provision of the agreement, such as its duration, or the underpayment of one party or overpayment by the other. This is a good practice to adopt in modifying this form agreement for your own use. The period of the license may be as short or as long (up to a maximum of the remainder of the term of copyright protection for the Work) as the parties wish. Use "for the full term of copyright protection" to license the copyright for the remainder of the term of copyright protection; otherwise, specify the number of months or years the license will endure.

13. Since a copyright owner may grant simultaneous exclusive licenses to a copyright in different geographic areas, specify the territory to which the license applies. If the Author's intent is to grant an exclusive license for the entire world, use this language: "That the Licensee shall have the right to exercise the rights granted herein throughout the world . . ."

14. Unless permission to alter the work is given by the Author of the work, anyone who significantly modifies it may be legally liable to the Author for distorting his or her work. This paragraph may be omitted if the Author objects to any modification of the Work. Or, any such modification may be made dependent upon the prior written approval of the Author: "That the Licensee shall not have the right to crop, edit, alter, or otherwise modify the work without the prior written consent of the Author to any such modification."

15. If payment is to be made in installments, use language similar to the following: "That the Licensee will pay to the Author the sum of ten thousand dollars ($10,000), which amount it is agreed will constitute the Author's only compensation for the grant of rights made herein and which shall be paid according to the following schedule: five thousand dollars ($5,000) shall be paid upon the execution of this agreement; twenty-five hundred dollars ($2,500) shall be paid on a date not later than thirty days after the date of execution of this agreement; and twenty-five hundred dollars ($2,500) shall be paid on a date not later than sixty days after the

date of execution of this agreement." The phrase "only compensation" refers to the fact that this agreement does not provide for the periodic payment of royalties to the Author, as do many agreements in which authors license copyrights to others, such as book publishers or music publishers. This simple form Exclusive License of Copyright is inadequate to document a license of copyright made in return for the promise of the payment of royalties; while the *license* provisions of this agreement are adequate for such an arrangement, agreements that provide for the payment of royalties universally make many other provisions, such as a provision specifying the right of the author to occasionally examine the books of the Licensee.

16. This sort of provision is common in licenses of copyright to protect the person or company acquiring the license of copyright from lawsuits for infringement based on actions of the Author. This seems reasonable if you consider that licensees usually have no knowledge of the circumstances surrounding the creation of the work of others and need to make sure that they are buying only rights in copyrights, *not* lawsuits.

17. This is called a "hold harmless" clause and is very common in book publishing, music publishing, and other agreements in which one party acquires rights in the copyright in a work created by an independent contractor. This is a fairly mild example of a hold harmless clause. Authors should expect to see provisions similar to those made in Paragraph 4 of this agreement in any document that exclusively licenses a copyright for any substantial period of time; no licensee should agree to acquire an exclusive license of copyright unless the author of the work will make, in writing, promises similar to these in the document that grants the license of copyright.

18. Insert the name of the state where you live here. It is an advantage to a litigant to be able to file or defend a suit in his or her home state. However, it may be that each party to the agreement will want any suit concerning it be filed in his or her home state. This is a point of negotiation but, as a practical matter, the more powerful of the two parties to the agreement will prevail.

19. This allows the Author to assign any sums due under the agreement to a third party or the estate of an Author who dies to collect any such sums on his or her behalf. It also permits the Licensee to in turn assign its exclusive license to another person or company. However, under some circumstances, especially those where the license is granted in return for the periodic payment of royalties, the Author will not want the Licensee to

assign its exclusive license to any other party; the usual reason for this objection is that the Author may not know and trust this secondary licensee and may have no confidence in the ability of any such secondary licensee to exploit the copyright in the Work. In such an event, add this language to limit the right of the Licensee to assign the license of copyright to another entity: "However, the Licensee shall not attempt to convey any of the rights granted herein to the Licensee by the Author to any third party without the prior written consent of the Author."

20. Specify how many original copies of the agreement (i.e., copies of the agreement, even if they are photocopies) there are that bear the original signatures of the parties.

21. In agreements, "as of" means: "We are signing this agreement today, but we mean for it to take effect *as of* two weeks ago, or next month." A date specified that is before or after the agreement is actually signed is referred to as the "effective date" of the agreement.

22. If you want the agreement to become effective on the date it is signed, use that date here. If you want it to be effective as of a previous date, use that date. If you want to postpone the time when the agreement becomes operative until a later date, use that future date.

23. Leave this space blank for the signature of the Author.

24. Leave this space blank for the signature of the Licensee.

25. Insert the Author's address here.

26. Insert the Licensee's address here.

27. Insert here the name of a person who is acting on behalf of his or her company when that company is the Licensee. If the Licensee is an individual, this line may be omitted.

28. It may be necessary for the Licensee to file a report of the Licensee's payments to the Author with the Internal Revenue Service; if so, the Author's Social Security Number will be necessary for any such filings.

29. Insert here the title of a person who is acting on behalf of his or her company when that company is the Licensee. If the Licensee is an individual, this line may be omitted.

FORM NON-EXCLUSIVE LICENSE OF COPYRIGHT

Although exclusive licenses of copyright must be in writing, it is not necessary that non-exclusive licenses of copyright be written. However, a written non-exclusive license is an excellent idea, if for no other reason than that the parties to the agreement will have documentation of the duration and scope of the license, as well as of other important terms of their agreement. This form agreement allows the author of a work to license it to another person or company on a non-exclusive basis—that is, other users of the copyright may be granted the same rights by the owner of the copyright.

Non-Exclusive License of Copyright

This agreement is made between Aaron Bowers[1] (hereinafter referred to as "the Author"[2]) and Ace Publishing Company[3] (hereinafter referred to as "the Licensee"), with reference to the following facts:

That the Author, an independent contractor,[4] is the creator of and owner of the copyright in a certain unpublished[5] drawing[6] (hereinafter referred to as "the Work"), which may be more fully described as follows:[7]

A three-by-five-inch pen-and-ink portrait of the poet Seamus Heaney, a photocopy[8] of which is attached hereto and made a part of this agreement by this reference.

The Author and the Licensee agree as follows:

1. That the Author hereby grants to the Licensee the non-exclusive right to reproduce, publish, prepare derivative works of and from, combine with other materials, display publicly, and otherwise use, control the use of, and exploit the Work[9] for a period of thirty-six (36)[10] months from the date written below.

2. That, during the term of this License of Copyright, the Licensee shall have the non-exclusive right to exercise the rights granted herein throughout the United States and Canada.[11]

3. That the Licensee shall have the right to crop, edit, alter, or otherwise modify the Work to the extent that the Licensee, in his or her sole discretion, deems necessary to suit it to such uses as the Licensee may choose to make of the Work.[12]

4. That the Licensee will pay to the Author the sum of five hundred dollars ($500), which amount it is agreed will constitute Author's only compensation for the grant of rights made herein.[13]

5. That the Author warrants that he or she is the owner of copyright in the Work and possesses full right and authority to convey the rights herein conveyed. The Author further warrants that the Work does not infringe the

copyright in any other work, and does not invade any privacy, publicity, trademark, or other rights of any other person.[14] The Author further agrees to indemnify and hold the Licensee harmless in any litigation in which a third party challenges any of the warranties made by the Author in this paragraph if any such litigation results in a judgment adverse to the Author in a court of competent jurisdiction;[15] and

6. That this agreement shall be governed by the laws of the State of Tennessee[16] applicable to contracts made and to be performed therein and shall be construed according to the Copyright Law of the United States, Title 17, Section 101, *et seq.,* United States Code; and

7. That this agreement shall inure to the benefit of and bind the parties and their respective heirs, representatives, successors, and assigns.[17]

In witness whereof, the Author and the Licensee have executed this document in two (2) counterpart originals[18] as of[19] the fifth day of September, 1996.[20]

_____ [21]	_____ [22]
AUTHOR	LICENSEE
_____ [23]	_____ [24]
ADDRESS	ADDRESS
_____	_____
_____	BY: _____ [25]
SOCIAL SECURITY NUMBER[26]	
	_____
	TITLE[27]

FORM NON-EXCLUSIVE LICENSE OF COPYRIGHT: NOTES

1. Insert the name of the author of the work. If two or more people created the work as co-authors, insert all their names here and add enough spaces for their signatures, etc., at the end of the agreement.

2. If you want to be more specific, use "Photographer," "Writer," "Songwriter," "Composer," "Illustrator," etc.; use the same designation throughout the document everywhere the word "Author" appears here. If two or more people created the work as co-authors, use the following language: "(hereinafter jointly referred to as 'the Author')."

3. Insert the name of the person or company to whom the copyright in the work is being licensed.

4. This form license agreement is inappropriate for use by anyone who is *not* an independent contractor. The works created by employees as part of their jobs are works-for-hire; no written agreement is necessary to document the work-for-hire situation in such a circumstance because the relationship of the employee and employer determines, as a matter of law, the ownership of the copyright in any work created on the job by the employee. However, even someone who works at a full-time job is an independent contractor with regard to any activity outside his or her job responsibilities. This language makes clear that the Author is not an employee of the Licensee.

5. If the Work has been published, use language similar to the following to specify the year of first publication of the Work: "a certain drawing, first published in 1996." One of the three elements of copyright notice is the year date of first publication of the work. (See chapter 2 for more information about copyright notice.)

6. Use an appropriate short designation for the type of work that is the subject of the assignment, i.e., "a photograph of three-year-old twin girls, each holding a black Labrador puppy," "a poem titled *Midsummer's Eve*," "a musical composition titled *Wind Dance*," "a short story titled 'High Hopes,'" "a non-fiction book manuscript titled *Butterflies of the Eastern States*," etc.

7. Insert a detailed description of the Work sufficient to allow the parties to the license and everyone else to determine just which particular work, out of all similar works, is the subject of the license.

8. If it is practicable, attach a copy of the Work, similar to the sort of copies required for registration of copyright, to each original of the Non-Exclusive License of Copyright document. If it is not practicable to do so, omit this language and use a much more detailed description of the Work or use photographs (for three-dimensional works such as sculptures) or other identifying material, such as the script for a film, and change the language describing the attached materials.

9. These are the exclusive rights of copyright given to copyright owners by the U.S. copyright statute and the copyright statutes of other countries. However, since this is a non-exclusive license, the Author may also grant the right to other parties to exercise these rights; further, the Author retains the right to exercise these rights simultaneously with any licensee.

10. When they draft agreements, lawyers traditionally use both words and figures to specify important numbers and sums of money one party must pay the other. This is done to diminish the possibility that a typographical error will lead to a misunderstanding of some important provision of the agreement, such as its duration, or the underpayment of one party or overpayment by the other. This is a good practice to adopt in modifying this form agreement for your own use. The period of the license may be as short or as long (up to a maximum of the remainder of the term of copyright protection for the Work) as the parties wish. Use "for the full term of copyright protection" to license the copyright for the remainder of the term of copyright protection; otherwise, specify the number of months or years the license will endure.

11. Specify the territory to which the license applies. If the Author's intent is to grant a non-exclusive license for the entire world, use this language: "That the Licensee shall have the non-exclusive right to exercise the rights granted herein throughout the world . . ."

12. Unless permission to alter the work is given by the Author of the work, anyone who significantly modifies it may be legally liable to the Author for distorting his or her work. This paragraph may be omitted if the Author objects to any modification of the Work. Or, any such modification may be made dependent upon the prior written approval of the Author: "That the Licensee shall not have the right to crop, edit, alter, or otherwise modify the work without the prior written consent of the Author to any such modification."

13. If payment is to be made in installments, use language similar to the following: "That the Licensee will pay to the Author the sum of ten thousand dollars ($10,000), which amount it is agreed will constitute the Author's only compensation for the grant of rights made herein and which shall be paid according to the following schedule: five thousand dollars ($5,000) shall be paid upon the execution of this agreement; twenty-five hundred dollars ($2,500) shall be paid on a date not later than thirty days after the date of execution of this agreement; and twenty-five hundred dollars ($2,500) shall be paid on a date not later than sixty days after the date of execution of this agreement." The phrase "only compensation" refers to the fact that this agreement does not provide for the periodic payment of royalties to the Author, as do many agreements in which authors license copyrights to others, such as book publishers or music publishers. This simple form Non-Exclusive License of Copyright is inadequate to

document a license of copyright made in return for the promise of the payment of royalties.

14. This sort of provision is common in licenses of copyright to protect the person or company acquiring the license of copyright from lawsuits for infringement based on actions of the Author. This seems reasonable if you consider that licensees usually have no knowledge of the circumstances surrounding the creation of the work of others and need to make sure that they are buying only rights in copyrights, not lawsuits.

15. This is called a "hold harmless" clause and is very common in book publishing, music publishing, and other agreements in which one party acquires rights in the copyright in a work created by an independent contractor. This is a fairly mild example of a hold harmless clause. Authors should expect to see provisions similar to those made in Paragraph 4 of this agreement in any document that licenses a copyright for any substantial period of time; no licensee should agree to acquire an license of copyright unless the author of the work will make, in writing, promises similar to these in the document that grants the license of copyright.

16. Insert the name of the state where you live here. It is an advantage to a litigant to be able to file or defend a suit in his or her home state. However, it may be that each party to the agreement will want any suit concerning it be filed in his or her home state. This is a point of negotiation but, as a practical matter, the more powerful of the two parties to the agreement will prevail.

17. This allows the Author to assign any sums due under the agreement to a third party or the estate of an Author who dies to collect any such sums on his or her behalf. It also permits the Licensee to, in turn, assign its non-exclusive license to another person or company. However, under some circumstances, especially those where the license is granted in return for the periodic payment of royalties, the Author will not want the Licensee to assign its non-exclusive license to any other party; the usual reason for this objection is that the Author may not know and trust this secondary licensee and may have no confidence in the ability of any such secondary licensee to exploit the copyright in the Work. In such an event, add this language to limit the right of the Licensee to assign the license of copyright to another entity: "However, the Licensee shall not attempt to convey any of the rights granted herein to the Licensee by the Author to any third party without the prior written consent of the Author."

18. Specify how many original copies of the agreement (i.e., copies of

the agreement, even if they are photocopies) there are that bear the original signatures of the parties.

19. In agreements, "as of" means: "We are signing this agreement today, but we mean for it to take effect *as of* two weeks ago, or next month." A date specified that is before or after the agreement is actually signed is referred to as the "effective date" of the agreement.

20. If you want the agreement to become effective on the date it is signed, use that date here. If you want it to be effective as of a previous date, use that date. If you want to postpone the time when the agreement becomes operative until a later date, use that future date.

21. Leave this space blank for the signature of the Author.

22. Leave this space blank for the signature of the Licensee.

23. Insert the Author's address here.

24. Insert the Licensee's address here.

25. Insert here the name of a person who is acting on behalf of his or her company when that company is the Licensee. If the Licensee is an individual, this line may be omitted.

26. It may be necessary for the Licensee to file a report of the Licensee's payments to the Author with the Internal Revenue Service; if so, the Author's Social Security Number will be necessary for any such filings.

27. Insert here the title of a person who is acting on behalf of his or her company when that company is the Licensee. If the Licensee is an individual, this line may be omitted.

FORM WORK-FOR-HIRE AGREEMENT

To be legally effective, work-for-hire agreements must be in writing and must be signed by both the creator of the specially commissioned work and the person or company that commissioned the work. For information about the situations in which work-for-hire agreements are appropriate, see chapter 4.

Work-For-Hire Agreement

This agreement is made between Rob Wilson[1] (hereinafter referred to as "the Illustrator"[2]) and Ace Publishing Company[3] (hereinafter referred to as "the Commissioning Party"), with reference to the following facts:

A. That the Illustrator, an independent contractor,[4] has prepared, at the instruction and under the direction of the Commissioning Party, a certain unpublished[5] drawing[6] (hereinafter referred to as "the Work"), which may be more fully described as follows:[7]

A three-by-five-inch pen-and-ink portrait of the poet Seamus Heaney, a photocopy[8] of which is attached hereto and made a part of this agreement by this reference.

B. That the Work was completed during 1996.[9]

C. That the Illustrator's date of birth is July 7, 1951.[10]

The Illustrator and the Commissioning Party agree as follows:

1. That the Work, including every embodiment thereof, was specifically prepared for the Commissioning Party and constitutes a work-for-hire, as defined in Title 17, Section 101, *et seq.,* United States Code, the Copyright Law of the United States. The Illustrator acknowledges and agrees that the Commissioning Party is and will be considered the author of the Work for purposes of copyright and is the owner of all rights of copyright in and to the Work and that the Commissioning Party will have the exclusive right to exercise all rights of copyright specified in Title 17, Section 101, *et seq.,* United States Code, the Copyright Law of the United States, for the full term of copyright and will be entitled to register the copyright in and to the Work in the Commissioning Party's name.

3. That the Commissioning Party will pay to the Illustrator the sum of five hundred dollars ($500),[11] which amount[12] it is agreed will constitute Illustrator's entire fee and only compensation[13] for the Illustrator's services in creating and preparing the Work and for the agreement made herein (excluding reimbursement for such reasonable expenses as may have been incurred by the Illustrator in connection with the creation of the Work) within thirty (30) days after delivery to the Commissioning Party of all existing physical embodiments of the Work, with the exception of a limited number of copies of the Work which the Illustrator may retain for the sole purpose of display in the Illustrator's professional portfolio or place of business or for entry in shows or competitions.[14]

4. That this agreement shall be governed by the laws of the State of Tennessee[15] applicable to contracts made and to be performed therein and shall be construed according to the Copyright Law of the United States, Title 17, Section 101, *et seq.,* United States Code; and

5. That this agreement shall inure to the benefit of and bind the parties and their respective heirs, representatives, successors, and assigns.[16]

In witness whereof, the Illustrator and the Commissioning Party have executed this document in two (2) counterpart originals[17] as of[18] the fifth day of September, 1996.[19]

_____ 20	_____ 21
ILLUSTRATOR	COMMISSIONING PARTY
_____ 22	_____ 23
ADDRESS	ADDRESS
_____	_____
_____	BY: _____ 24
SOCIAL SECURITY NUMBER[25]	
	_____
	TITLE[26]

FORM WORK-FOR-HIRE AGREEMENT: NOTES

1. Insert the name of the Illustrator of the work. If two or more people created the work as co-authors, insert all their names here and add enough spaces for their signatures, etc., at the end of the agreement.

2. In every other situation where the creator of a work conveys the copyright in the work to another party, that creator is forever considered the author of the work, even after the copyright is owned by someone else. With a work-for-hire, the entity that commissions the work is considered, for copyright purposes, the "author" of the work from the inception of the work. Therefore, in this work-for-hire agreement, it is preferable to use a term other than "Author" to designate the creator of the Work. The best approach is to refer to the creator by a name that describes his or her profession, i.e., use "Photographer," "Writer," "Songwriter," "Composer," etc. Use the same designation throughout the document to refer to the creator of the work. If two or more people created the work as co-authors, use the following language: "(hereinafter jointly referred to as 'the Songwriters')."

3. Insert the name of the person or company that commissioned the Work.

4. This form work-for-hire agreement is inappropriate for use by anyone who is *not* an independent contractor. The works created by employees as

a part of their jobs are works-for-hire; no written agreement is necessary to document the work-for-hire situation in such a circumstance because the relationship of the employee and employer determines, as a matter of law, the ownership of the copyright in any work created on the job by the employee. However, even someone who works at a full-time job is an independent contractor with regard to any activity outside his or her job responsibilities.

5. If the Work has been published, use language similar to the following to specify the year of first publication of the Work: "a certain drawing, first published in 1996." One of the three elements of copyright notice is the year date of first publication of the work. (See chapter 2 for more information about copyright notice.)

6. Use an appropriate short designation for the type of work that is the subject of the Work-For-Hire Agreement, i.e., "a photograph of three-year-old twin girls, each holding a black Labrador puppy," "a poem titled *Midsummer's Eve*," "a musical composition titled *Wind Dance*," "a short story titled 'High Hopes,'" "a non-fiction book manuscript titled *Butterflies of the Eastern States*," etc.

7. Insert a detailed description of the Work sufficient to allow the parties to the agreement and everyone else to determine just which particular work, out of all similar works, is the subject of the agreement.

8. If it is practicable, attach a copy of the Work, similar to the sort of copies required for registration of copyright, to each original of the Work-For-Hire Agreement document. If it is not practicable to do so, omit this language and use a much more detailed description of the Work or use photographs (for three-dimensional works such as sculptures) or other identifying material, such as the script for a film, and change the language describing the attached materials.

9. Specify the year during which the Work was finished by the Illustrator. (This year date is required on any application for copyright registration.)

10. Insert the correct date. (The Author's date of birth is also required on any application for copyright registration.)

11. When they draft agreements, lawyers traditionally use both words and figures to specify sums of money one party must pay the other. This is done to diminish the possibility that a typographical error will lead to the underpayment of one party or overpayment by the other. It is a good rule to follow in modifying this form agreement for your own use.

12. If payment is to be made in installments, use language similar to

the following: "That the Commissioning Party will pay to the Illustrator the sum of ten thousand dollars ($10,000), which amount it is agreed will constitute the Illustrator's entire fee and only compensation for the Illustrator's services in creating and preparing the Work and for the agreement made herein (excluding reimbursement for such reasonable expenses as may have been incurred by the Illustrator in connection with the creation of the Work) and which shall be paid according to the following schedule: five thousand dollars ($5,000) shall be paid upon the execution of this agreement; twenty-five hundred dollars ($2,500) shall be paid on a date not later than thirty days after the date of execution of this agreement; and twenty-five hundred dollars ($2,500) shall be paid on a date not later than sixty days after the date of execution of this agreement."

13. The phrase "entire fee and only compensation" refers to the fact that this agreement does not provide for the periodic payment of royalties to the Illustrator, as do some other agreements in which authors transfer copyrights to others, such as book publishers or music publishers. This Work-For-Hire Agreement is inappropriate for use in any such situation.

14. Although the Commissioning Party will own the copyright in the Work, it is considerate to allow the Illustrator of the Work to retain a few copies of the work, if that is possible. This courtesy to the Illustrator does not diminish or endanger the rights of the Commissioning Party since ownership of a physical object that embodies a work conveys no rights in the copyright in the work. The Illustrator can look at and show the retained copies of the Work, but cannot make any further copies or otherwise exercise any rights of copyright.

15. Insert the name of the state where you live here. It is an advantage to a litigant to be able to file or defend a suit in his or her home state. However, it may be that each party to the agreement will want any suit concerning it be filed in his or her home state. This is a point of negotiation but, as a practical matter, the more powerful of the two parties to the agreement will prevail.

16. This allows the Illustrator to assign any sums due under the agreement to a third party or the estate of an Illustrator who dies to collect any such sums on his or her behalf.

17. Specify how many original copies of the agreement (i.e., copies of the agreement, even if they are photocopies) there are that bear the original signatures of the parties.

18. In agreements, "as of" means: "We are signing this agreement

today, but we mean for it to take effect *as of* two weeks ago, or next month." A date specified that is before or after the agreement is actually signed is referred to as the "effective date" of the agreement.

19. If you want the agreement to become effective on the date it is signed, use that date here. If you want it to be effective as of a previous date, use that date. If you want to postpone the time when the agreement becomes operative until a later date, use that future date.

20. Leave this space blank for the signature of the Illustrator.

21. Leave this space blank for the signature of the Commissioning Party.

22. Insert the Illustrator's address here.

23. Insert the Commissioning Party's address here.

24. Insert here the name of a person who is acting on behalf of his or her company when that company is the Commissioning Party. If the Commissioning Party is an individual, this line may be omitted.

25. It may be necessary for the Commissioning Party to file a report of its payments to the Illustrator with the Internal Revenue Service; if so, the Illustrator's Social Security Number will be necessary for any such filings.

26. Insert here the title of a person who is acting on behalf of his or her company when that company is the Commissioning Party. If the Commissioning Party is an individual, this line may be omitted.

Glossary

access The first element of the three-part test for copyright infringement. That is, in a case for infringement of a novel, did the defendant have access to the manuscript or a published version of the plaintiff's book so that copying was possible? Usually access must be proved before the other two parts of the copyright test (copying of protected expression and substantial similarity) are considered.

actual damages The profits a copyright infringer made from the infringing work and the money the plaintiff lost because of the infringement. A court deciding a copyright infringement case may award either actual damages or statutory damages.

anonymous work A work on the copies or phonorecords of which no natural person is identified as author.

assignment of copyright Like a sale of a copyright, usually made in return for a lump sum payment or the promise of the payment of a share of the income produced by the work. For example, in the case of a music publishing agreement, a transfer of ownership of the song copyright from the songwriter to the music publisher is made in return for the promises the publisher makes in the music publishing agreement regarding advance and periodic payments of royalties to the author. In addition to assignment of an entire copyright, an author may also assign only part of a copyright. The copyright statute requires that the transfer of ownership of any copyright be made in a written document signed by the person assigning the ownership of the copyright to someone else; no verbal assignment of copyright is possible. Anyone who acquires any right of copyright by assignment can, in turn, sell that right to someone else unless the written assignment document provides otherwise. An assignment of copyright may also be referred to as a "transfer" of copyright. Assignment of copyright is one of three ways that ownership of rights in copyright is transferred to someone besides the author of the copyrighted work; the other two are license and work-for-hire.

audiovisual work A work that consists of a series of related images which are intrinsically intended to be shown by the use of machines or devices such as projectors, viewers, or electronic equipment, together with accompanying sounds, if any, regardless of the nature of the material objects, such as films or tapes, in which the works are embodied.

author In the language of the U.S. copyright statute, the creator of any copyrightable work, whether that work is a book, photograph, painting, poem, play, musical composition, or other sort of work. The exception to this is work-for-hire; if a work is created as a work-for-hire, the employer of the creator of the copyright owns the copyright from the inception of the work and is considered the author of the work for purposes of copyright.

Berne Convention The Convention for the Protection of Literary and Artistic Works, signed at Berne, Switzerland, on September 9, 1886, and all acts, protocols, and revisions thereto.
   A work is a "Berne Convention work" if:

1. in the case of an unpublished work, one or more of the authors is a national of a nation adhering to the Berne Convention, or in the case of a published work, one or more of the authors is a national of a nation adhering to the Berne Convention on the date of first publication;
2. the work was first published in a nation adhering to the Berne Convention, or was simultaneously first published in a nation adhering to the Berne Convention and in a foreign nation that does not adhere to the Berne Convention;
3. in the case of an audiovisual work—(a) if one or more of the authors is a legal entity, that author has its headquarters in a nation adhering to the Berne Convention; or (b) if one or more of the authors is an individual, that author is domiciled, or has his or her habitual residence in, a nation adhering to the Berne Convention;
4. in the case of a pictorial, graphic, or sculptural work that is incorporated in a building or other structure, the building or structure is located in a nation adhering to the Berne Convention; or
5. in the case of an architectural work embodied in a building, such building is erected in a country adhering to the Berne Convention.

For purposes of Paragraph 1, an author who is domiciled in or has his or her habitual residence in, a nation adhering to the Berne Convention is considered to be a national of that nation. For purposes of Paragraph 2, a work is considered to have been simultaneously published in two or more nations if its dates of publication are within thirty days of one another.

best edition   The "best edition" of a work is the edition, published in the United States at any time before the date of deposit, that the Library of Congress determines to be most suitable for its purposes. This usually means the best quality version of the work available at the time registration is applied for.

case law   Law that originates in the decisions of courts as opposed to written laws passed by state legislatures or the U.S. Congress, which are called "statutes."

cease and desist letter   A letter written by the lawyer for the plaintiff telling the defendant to immediately cease certain specified actions that infringe the plaintiff's copyright and thereafter desist from any further such actions. These letters are usually the first indication that a defendant has that his or her actions may have violated the plaintiff's rights. Depending on the merits of the plaintiff's claims of infringement, a defendant will decide to comply with the plaintiff's demands and try to settle the infringement dispute out of court or to fight the plaintiff's assertions of infringement in court.

children   According to the copyright statute, a person's "children" are that person's immediate offspring, whether legitimate or not, and any children legally adopted by that person.

collective work   A work, such as a periodical issue, anthology, or encyclopedia, in which a number of contributions, constituting separate and independent works in themselves, are assembled into a collective whole.

compilation   A work formed by the collection and assembling of pre-existing materials or of data that are selected, coordinated, or arranged in such a way that the resulting work as a whole constitutes an original work of authorship. The term "compilation" includes collective works.

constructive notice   The presumption that because a copyright registration is reflected in the records of the Copyright Office, which are public, everyone knows of the claim of copyright ownership the registration embodies, regardless of whether any examination of those records is actually made.

contingency fee   A lawyer's fee taken from an award of damages to the plaintiff. Copyright infringement suits are often filed by lawyers who agree to work for a contingency fee; that is, the lawyer agrees that the fee for his or her work is to be taken from and is contingent upon an award by the court in favor of the plaintiff. If the plaintiff loses, the lawyer is not paid a fee. In any event, a plaintiff is still responsible for bearing the costs of the suit, such as his or her lawyer's travel expenses, the costs of court reporters for depositions, and the fees of expert witnesses. Lawyers never agree to work on a contingency fee basis for defendants who have no expectation of any awards.

copies Material objects, other than phonorecords, in which a work is fixed by any method now known or later developed, and from which the work can be perceived, reproduced, or otherwise communicated, either directly or with the aid of a machine or device. The term "copies" includes the material object, other than a phonorecord, in which the work is first fixed.

copying The second part of the three-part test for copyright infringement. That is, was part of the protected expression of the plaintiff's work copied by the defendant? Usually a defendant must be found to have copied significant portions of the plaintiff's work before this part of the copyright infringement test is satisfied. The mere fact that two works share certain similarities, even if those similarities are significant, is not sufficient to prove infringement unless the defendant copied from the plaintiff's work. Coincidental creation of a similar work, without copying, is not actionable under the U.S. copyright statute, even if the works in question are so similar as to be nearly identical.

copyright The set of exclusive rights that are granted, initially to the creators of copyrightable works, by the various copyright statutes that exist in most countries.

copyright infringement The unauthorized exercise of any of the exclusive rights reserved by law to copyright owners. The most usual sort of copyright infringement lawsuit claims that the defendant is guilty of unauthorized copying from the plaintiff's work. In this situation, copyright infringement is judged by a three-part circumstantial evidence test: (1) Did the accused infringer have access to the work that is said to have been infringed, in order to make copying possible? (2) Is the defendant actually guilty of copying from the plaintiff's work part of the plaintiff's protectable expression? and (3) Is the accused work substantially similar to the work the plaintiff says was copied? Coincidental creation of a work similar to an existing copyrighted work is not infringement; the gist of most copyright infringements is unauthorized copying.

copyright notice   The three elements that legally serve to give notice to the world that a copyright owner is claiming ownership of a particular work. Copyright notice consists of three parts: the word "copyright" or the © symbol (or, for sound recordings, the ℗ symbol), the year of first publication of the work, and the name of the copyright owner. No formalities are required to use copyright notice, and although it is no longer required to secure copyright protection, use of copyright notice does confer certain valuable procedural benefits (in a copyright infringement lawsuit) on the copyright owner.

copyright protection   The protection the law gives copyright owners from unauthorized use of their works during the term of copyright.

copyright registration   The registration of a claim to ownership of a copyright, made in Washington, D.C., in the U.S. Copyright Office, a division of the Library of Congress. Copyright registration enhances the rights an author gains automatically by the act of creating a copyrightable work but does not, of itself, create these rights. The Copyright Office prescribes a specific form for the registration of copyright in each particular variety of work. Form TX is used for the registration of "literary" works, that is works, other than dramatic works, that consist primarily of TeXtual matter. Form VA is used to register copyrights in works of the Performing Arts, including plays, songs, and movies. Form SR is used to register the copyrights in Sound Recordings. There are other forms for other sorts of works; the name of the major varieties of copyright registration forms and the sort of works to be registered with each are listed in chapter 4.

copyright statute   In the United States, the written copyright law passed by Congress, as opposed to copyright law that originates in the decisions of courts, which is called "case law." The current United States copyright statute became effective January 1, 1978 and changed significantly many aspects of copyright law operative under the previous statute. Because the copyright statute is a federal statute and federal law outranks state law, there is no such thing as a state copyright statute. Most other countries also have copyright statutes, the provisions of which often vary from those of the U.S. statute.

creation   A work is created when it is fixed in a copy or phonorecord for the first time; where a work is prepared over a period of time, the portion of it that has been fixed at any particular time constitutes the work as of that time, and where the work has been prepared in different versions, each version constitutes a separate work.

criminal copyright infringement   Any person who infringes a copyright willfully and for purposes of commercial advantage or private financial gain may be punished by a court as a criminal infringer of copyright. Penalties may include fines or forfeiture and destruction of copies of the infringed work (or other disposition, such as transferring ownership of the infringing copies to the plaintiff).

defendant   The person or company whose actions are complained of in a lawsuit. In criminal trials, a defendant is presumed innocent until proven guilty. In civil lawsuits, such as a suit for copyright infringement, no such presumption is made. Nothing is presumed about the actions of either the defendant and the plaintiff (the person or company that files the suit) until it is proven to the court. This means that even an innocent defendant is in the same position as a plaintiff, i.e., the defendant must prove his or her innocence just as the plaintiff must try to prove the truth of the allegations made in the complaint.

defenses   The arguments a defendant in a lawsuit makes in self-defense. The most important and the most commonly used defense in copyright infringement suits is the defense of "fair use," which is the argument that the complained-of actions by the defendant are allowable under the law as a permitted use of the plaintiff's work.

deposit copies   Copies of the "best edition" of a work that are required to be deposited with the Copyright Office as a part of an application for copyright registration. The copyright statute requires that copies of works first published in the United States with copyright notice be deposited with the Copyright Office even if no application for copyright registration is made. Copyright registration forms give information on what sort of copies and how many copies of a work should accompany the application for registration of that work. The Copyright Office also publishes a free pamphlet concerning mandatory deposit of copies.

derivative work   An alternate version of a copyrighted work, i.e., a work "derived" from or based upon one or more pre-existing works, such as a translation, musical arrangement, dramatization, fictionalization, motion picture version, sound recording, art reproduction, abridgment, condensation, or any other form in which a work may be recast, transformed, or adapted. A work consisting of editorial revisions, annotations, elaborations, or other modifications, which as a whole, represent an original work of authorship, is a derivative work. The right to prepare derivative works from a copyrighted work is one of the exclusive rights of copyright reserved to copyright owners in the U.S. copyright statute.

display   To display a work means to show a copy of it, either directly or by means of a film, slide, television image, or any other device or process or, in the case of a motion picture or other audiovisual work, to show individual images nonsequentially. This right is becoming increasingly important to copyright owners as varieties of works for which the display right has never before been important, such as text works, are put into digital form for display on the Internet.

exclusive rights of copyright   Those rights pertaining to a copyright that may be exercised only, or exclusively, by the owner of that copyright. Under the United States copyright statute, the creator of a copyrighted creative work has the exclusive right to copy or reproduce the work, to prepare alternate or "derivative" versions of the work, to distribute and sell copies of the work, and to perform or display the work publicly. Usually these rights may not be exercised by anyone other than the author of the work or a person to whom he or she has sold or licensed one or more of these "exclusive rights."

exploitation of copyright   The use of a work to produce income. Book publishers exploit book copyrights. Song copyrights are exploited by music publishers; the copyrights in recorded performances of songs are exploited by record companies. Copyrights in plays and film scripts are exploited by theater and movie producers.

expression   Copyright subsists only in the expression embodied in a work and not in the underlying ideas upon which the work is based. The copyright statute specifically limits copyright protection to works that embody some expression and excludes from protection a list of various products of the imagination that do not embody sufficient expression to qualify for protection: "[i]n no case does copyright protection for an original work of authorship extend to any idea, procedure, process, system, method of operation, concept, principle, or discovery, regardless of the form in which it is described, explained, illustrated, or embodied in such work."

"fair use"   A kind of public-policy exception to the usual standard for determining copyright infringement; that is, there is an infringing use of a copyrighted work but because of a countervailing public interest, that use is permitted and is not called infringement. Any use that is deemed by the law to be "fair" typically creates some social, cultural, or political benefit which outweighs any resulting harm to the copyright owner. The copyright statute identifies six purposes that will qualify a use as a possible fair use: criticism, comment, news reporting, teaching, scholarship, or research. Once any use of a copyrighted work has been proved to have been made for one of these six purposes, the use must be examined to determine whether it is indeed fair. The copyright statute lists four factors that courts must weigh in determining fair use; the purpose and character of the use, including whether such use is of a commercial nature or is for non-profit educational purposes; the nature of the copyrighted work; the amount and substantiality of the portion used in relation to the copyrighted work as a whole; and the effect of the use upon the potential market for or value of the copyrighted work.

fixation   One of three statutory requirements for copyright protection; the other two are that the work must embody some "expression" of the author, rather than consisting only of an idea or ideas, and the work must be "original," that is, the work was not copied from another work. The U.S. copyright statute provides that the moment a work is "fixed" in any tangible form that allows the work to be perceived by the senses (with or without the aid of a mechanical device, such as a CD player or videocassette player), that work is automatically protected by copyright. A work is "fixed" in a tangible medium of expression when its embodiment in a copy or phonorecord, by or under the authority of the author, is sufficiently permanent or stable to permit it to be perceived, reproduced, or otherwise communicated for a period of more than transitory duration. A work consisting of sounds, images, or both, that are being transmitted, is considered by the copyright statute to be "fixed" if a fixation of the work is being made simultaneously with its transmission.

independent contractor   One who performs work for an employer but is not an employee of that employer. Another term for independent contractor is "freelance" or "freelancer." The status of one who creates a work is important to the determination whether that work is a work made for hire. Several factors are relevant to the evaluation of the status of the creator of a work *vis a vis* the party who commissions the work to be created: the skill required to produce the work; on whose premises the work will be produced; the duration of the relationship between the party who commissions the work and the person who will create it; whether the party who commissions the work has the right to assign additional projects to the person who will create the work; the extent of the discretion that may be exercised by the person who will create the work over when and how long he or she works during the process of creating it; the method by which the person who creates the work will be paid for his or her services; the role of the party who commissions the work in hiring and paying assistants for the person who will create the work; whether the work is part of the regular business of the party who commissions it; whether the party who commissions the work is in business; whether the party who commissions the work provides employee benefits to the person who will create the work; and the tax treatment of the person who will create the work.

injunction A court order that directs the enjoined party to do something, or more typically, to cease doing something and to refrain from doing it in future. Plaintiffs in copyright infringement suits typically seek injunctions to stop defendants from continuing to infringe the plaintiffs' copyrights. The scope of an injunction and whether a litigant's motion for one is granted is at the discretion of the judge who hears the suit. A temporary injunction is usually granted at the same time a suit is filed and endures only ten days. A preliminary injunction is granted by a judge after hearing arguments for and against the injunction from both the plaintiff and the defendant and usually lasts until the end of the lawsuit, when it may ripen into a permanent injunction by means of a paragraph to that effect in the judge's written order rendering his or her decision.

intellectual property Intangible property that is a product of the imagination, i.e., copyrights, trademarks, and patents. Although all three protect products of the human imagination, copyrights, trademarks, and patents are distinct but complementary. Each is governed by a different federal law and the principles concerning ownership, registration, and infringement of each vary widely.

joint work A work prepared by two or more authors with the intention that their contributions be merged into inseparable or interdependent parts of a unitary whole.

judgment The ruling of the judge, rendered at the conclusion of a lawsuit. Judgments in civil (as opposed to criminal) trials usually include an order that the defendant, if the defendant is found to be guilty of the actions that caused the plaintiff to sue, pay the plaintiff money damages and, sometimes, attorneys' fees. Judgments in copyright infringement cases may also include orders to destroy the defendant's infringing copies of the plaintiff's work and injunctions to prevent further infringing actions of the defendant.

license of copyright   If an assignment of copyright is like a sale of the copyright, a license of copyright is like a lease. A non-exclusive license of a copyright may be verbal, but an exclusive license is required by the copyright statute to be in writing.

literary work   A work, other than an audiovisual work, that is expressed in words, numbers, or other verbal or numerical symbols or indicia, regardless of the nature of the material object, such as a book, periodical, manuscript, phonorecord, film, tape, disk, or card, in which it is embodied.

non-disclosure letter   Also called a "non-disclosure agreement" or a "disclosure letter," a non-disclosure letter is a document used by the owner of a trade secret to create a legally enforceable contractual obligation to preserve the trade secret, which is disclosed to the person or company that signs the non-disclosure letter for the sole purpose of allowing that person or company to consider exploiting the trade secret under an arrangement whereby the owner of the trade secret would be compensated for its use.

ordinary observer test   The test courts use in determining whether substantial similarity exists in copyright infringement cases. Courts try to decide whether an ordinary observer would believe that the defendant's work and the plaintiff's work are the same. If so, substantial similarity, the third part of the three-part test for copyright infringement, exists.

originality   "Originality" means simply that a work was not copied from another work rather than that the work is unique or unusual. Originality is one of three statutory requirements for copyright protection; the other two are that the work must embody some "expression" of the author, rather than consisting only of an idea or ideas, and the work must be "fixed" in some tangible medium of expression. For purposes of copyright protection, if a work is not copied from another work, it is said to be original. Similarities between two works are immaterial so long as they do not result from copying.

parody A work that satirizes another work. A parody becomes infringement of the parodied work when it takes more from the parodied work than is absolutely necessary to call that work to mind.

patent The rights granted by the federal government to the originator of a physical invention or industrial or technical process (a "utility patent") or an ornamental design for an "article of manufacture" (a "design patent"). Utility patents last seventeen years; design patents last fourteen years.

perform To "perform" a work means to recite, render, play, dance, or act it, either directly or by means of any device or process or, in the case of a motion picture or other audiovisual work, to show its images in any sequence or to make the sounds accompanying it audible.

permission A consent to use a work, usually by reprinting or reproducing it in some other work, such as the reproduction of photographs in a biography of the subject of the photographs. Permissions are actually non-exclusive licenses to use a work in a specified way. The owner of copyright in the materials sought to be used may or may not be compensated for the use.

phonorecords Material objects in which sounds, other than those accompanying a motion pictures or other audiovisual work, are fixed by any method now known or later developed, and from which the sounds can be perceived, reproduced, or otherwise communicated, either directly or with the aid of a machine or device. The term "phonorecords" includes the material object in which the sounds are first fixed.

pictorial, graphic, and sculptural works Two-dimensional and three-dimensional works of fine, graphic, and applied art, photographs, prints and art reproductions, maps, globes, charts, diagrams, models, and technical drawings, including architectural plans. Such works shall include works of artistic craftsmanship insofar as their form but not their mechanical or utilitarian aspects are concerned; the design of a useful article shall be considered a pictorial, graphic, or sculptural work only if, and only to the extent that, such design incorporates pictorial, graphic, or sculptural features that can be identified separately from, and are capable of existing independently of, the utilitarian aspects of the article.

plaintiff   In a civil lawsuit, the person or company that files a lawsuit to complain of the actions of the defendant that the plaintiff believes violate the plaintiff's rights. In a copyright infringement lawsuit, the plaintiff asks the court to order the defendant to stop its infringing actions and asks for an award of money damages to compensate the plaintiff for the harm the defendant's actions caused.

protectable expression   Those elements of a work that are protected by copyright. The most basic premise of copyright law is that copyright does not protect ideas, only expressions of ideas. Therefore, the idea on which a copyrighted work is based is not granted protection under copyright law. Other unprotectable elements of otherwise copyrightable works are: *scènes à faire*; literary characters; titles of books, stories, poems, songs, movies, etc.; short phrases and slogans; the rhythm or structure of musical works; themes expressed by song lyrics, short musical phrases, arrangements of musical compositions that do not constitute an alternate versions of the compositions; social dance steps and simple routines; uses of color, perspective, geometric shapes, and standard arrangements dictated by aesthetic convention in works of the visual arts; jewelry designs that merely mimic the structures of nature; names of products, services, or businesses; pseudonyms or professional or stage names (names and titles may be protected under trademark law, however); mere variations on familiar symbols, emblems, or designs, such as typefaces, numerals, or punctuation symbols, and religious emblems or national symbols;

information, research data, and bare historical facts; blank forms, such as account ledger page forms, diaries, address books, blank checks, restaurant checks, order forms, and the like; and measuring and computing devices such as slide rules or tape measures; calendars, height and weight charts, sporting event schedules, and other assemblages of commonly available information that contain no original material; and raw information and bare historical facts (although many compilations of such information and extended expressions based on historical facts are protectable by copyright).

pseudonymous work   A work on the copies or phonorecords of which the author is identified under a fictitious name.

public domain   Primarily, works for which copyright protection has expired. The U.S. copyright statute is based on the assumption that creative people will be encouraged to be creative if they are given exclusive control for a period of time over the use of their works. After that control ends, the public benefits from the right to make unlimited use of the previously-protected creations. When a work falls into the public domain the work has become available for use in any way by anyone. Besides works for which copyright protection has expired, the other major category of public domain works is works created by officers or employees of the U.S. government as part of their government jobs, which are in the public domain because the government has chosen not to claim copyright in works created at the taxpayers' expense.

publication   The distribution of copies or phonorecords of a work to the public by sale or other transfer of ownership, or by rental, lease, or lending. The offering to distribute copies or phonorecords to a group of persons for purposes of further distribution, public performance, or public display, constitutes publication. A public performance or display of a work does not of itself constitute publication. To perform or display a work "publicly" means (1) to perform or display it at a place open to the public or at any place where a substantial number or persons outside of a normal circle of a family and its social acquaintances is gathered; or (2) to transmit or otherwise communicate a performance or display of the work to a place specified by clause (1) or to the public, by means of any device or process, whether the members of the public capable of receiving the performance or display receive it in the same place or in separate places and at the same time or at different times. Because publication, in the context of copyright, can determine the expiration of the term of copyright for a work created as a work-for-hire or under a pseudonym, it can be very important to determine whether and when such a work has been published within the meaning of the copyright statute.

recordation   The recording in the Copyright Office of the document that evidences an assignment of copyright or an exclusive license agreement. Recordation confers several benefits, such as creating a public record of a change in ownership in rights in a work and of the current ownership of those rights.

scènes à faire   Common literary or dramatic conventions such as the star-crossed lovers or the pauper who is actually the lost heir to a fortune. Such devices are a variety of idea and are therefore, in themselves, not protected by copyright, although particular expressions of these conventions are protectable.

settlement   Either the termination of a dispute or lawsuit by mutual agreement of the plaintiff and the defendant or the sum of money that is often paid, as an incentive to reach such an agreement, to the plaintiff by the defendant in lieu of any award of damages a court could make. The majority of lawsuits are settled before trial. The contract that embodies the agreement reached, in addition to providing for a payment to the plaintiff in settlement of the dispute or suit, may include promises by one party to do or in future refrain from doing something.

sound recordings   Works that result from the fixation of a series of musical, spoken, or other sounds, but not including the sounds accompanying a motion picture or other audiovisual work, regardless of the nature of the material objects, such as disks, tapes, or other phonorecords, in which they are embodied.

statute of limitations   The period within which a lawsuit must be filed. The statute of limitations for copyright infringement is three years from the date the infringer commits the infringing acts. In the case of a continuing infringement, the statute runs from the date of the defendant's last infringing act. After the three-year period has passed, an infringement suit will likely be barred by the court.

statutory damages   A range of money damages the copyright statute allows courts to award a plaintiff in a copyright infringement suit instead of the money lost by the plaintiff as a result of an infringer's actions plus the actual amount by which the infringer profited from the use of the plaintiff's work. Because actual damages can be very difficult, time-consuming, expensive, or impossible to prove during infringement lawsuits, and because infringers often do not profit from their infringements, awards of statutory damages are often desirable.

"striking similarity"   A specialized application of the three-part test for copyright infringement. In cases where the similarity between two works is so striking that there is no explanation for such overwhelming similarity other than that one work was copied from the other, courts say that the "access" portion of the three-part test may be assumed and that circumstances that made the infringement possible need not be reconstructed by the plaintiff. However, the "striking similarity" approach to proving infringement is rarely allowed by courts, which prefer to see plaintiffs prove every element of their cases.

substantial similarity   The third part of the three-part test for copyright infringement. That is, in a case for infringement, is the defendant's work substantially similar to the plaintiff's work? Substantial similarity is more than isolated, insignificant similarities, but the "infringed" work and the accused work need not be identical for substantial similarity to be found.

term of copyright   The period during which copyright protection endures for a copyrightable work. For any work created after December 31, 1977, copyright protection begins the moment the work is first fixed in a tangible form. How long it lasts depends to a large extent on who wrote it and under what circumstances. Under ordinary circumstances, copyright protection lasts for the remainder of the life of the author of the work plus fifty years; if two or more authors jointly create a work, copyright protection will endure until fifty years after the last of the authors dies. If a work is created as a work-for-hire, anonymously, or under a fictitious name, the term of copyright will be either one hundred years from the date the work was created or seventy-five years from the date it is published, whichever period expires first.

termination of transfers   A right given authors (and certain of their heirs) in the current U.S. copyright statute by which they may recover ownership of copyrights previously assigned or licensed to someone else thirty-five years after first publication of the work or forty years after the transfer is made, whichever comes first. The termination-of-transfers provisions of the statute specify precise procedures for exercising this right of recovery, and these procedures require that good records be kept of copyrights that are assigned to others. The rules for copyrights created before 1978 and those created after December 31, 1977 are significantly different. In most cases, consulting a copyright lawyer is an important step in ensuring that the required termination-of-transfers procedures are followed and the termination is effected.

trade secrets   Valuable formulas, patterns, compilations, programs, devices, methods, techniques, or processes, that are not generally known or discoverable and that are maintained in secrecy by their owners. Because copyright does not protect ideas, methods, systems, etc., trade secrets are usually unprotectable by copyright. Such secret information is preserved by the use of non-disclosure letters that obligate those to whom trade secrets are disclosed to keep them secret.

trademark   A word or symbol used to identify a product or service in the marketplace. Rights in a trademark accrue only by use of the trademark in commerce and belong to the company that applies the mark to its products rather than to the person who creates the name or logo. A company gains rights in a trademark in direct proportion to the geographic scope and duration of its use of the mark; ordinarily, the company that uses a mark first gains rights in that mark superior to those of any other company that later uses it for the same product or services. Unauthorized use of a mark is infringement.

transfer of copyright   Another term for assignment of copyright ownership. A transfer of copyright ownership is an assignment, mortgage, exclusive license, or any other conveyance, alienation, or hypothecation of a copyright or of any of the exclusive rights comprised in a copyright, whether or not it is limited in time or place of effect, but not including a nonexclusive license.

unpublished work   Any work that has not been distributed to the public by sale or other transfer of ownership, or by rental, lease, or lending. The offering to distribute copies or phonorecords to a group of persons for purposes of further distribution, public performance, or public display, constitutes publication. The law generally allows few "fair" uses of unpublished works than of published works.

useful article   An article having an intrinsic utilitarian function that is not merely to portray the appearance of the article or to convey information. An article that is normally a part of a useful article is considered a "useful article."

utilitarian elements of industrial design   The elements pictorial, graphic, and sculptural works that are specifically excluded from copyright protection in the copyright statute. Only the non-functional aspects of such works are protectable; generally, decorative elements of designs for useful articles are protected while the "mechanical or utilitarian aspects" of such designs are not.

widow or widower   The surviving spouse under the law of the author's domicile at the time of his or her death, whether or not the spouse has later remarried.

work   In the language of the U.S. copyright statute, any copyrightable product of the imagination, whether it is a book, photograph, painting, poem, play, musical composition, movie, or other sort of work.

work made for hire   A work created by an independent contractor (a freelancer) if the work falls into one of nine categories of specially commissioned works named in the U.S. copyright statute and both the independent contractor and the person who commissions the creation of the work agree in writing that it is to be considered a work-for-hire, or a work that is created by an employee as part of his or her full-time job. Works-made-for-hire belong to the employers of the people who create them, and those employers are considered the authors of those works for copyright purposes from the inception of the works. (Work-for-hire is one of three ways that ownership of rights in copyright are transferred to someone besides the author of the copyrighted work; the other two are assignment of copyright and license of copyright.)

work of visual art   A work of visual art is (1) a painting, drawing, print, or sculpture, existing in a single copy, in a limited edition of two hundred copies or fewer that are signed and consecutively numbered by the author, or, in the case of a sculpture, in multiple cast, carved, or fabricated sculptures of two hundred copies or fewer that are consecutively numbered by the author and bear the signature or other identifying mark of the author; or (2) a still photographic image produced for exhibition purposes only, existing in a single copy that is signed by the author, or in a limited edition of two hundred copies or fewer that are signed and consecutively numbered by the author.

A work of visual art does not include (A)(i) any poster, map, globe, chart, technical drawing, diagram, model, applied art, motion picture or other audiovisual work, book, magazine, newspaper, periodical, data base, electronic information service, electronic publication, or similar publication; (ii) any merchandising item or advertising, promotional, descriptive, covering, or packaging material or container; (iii) any portion or part of any item described above in this paragraph; (B) any work made for hire; or any work not subject to copyright protection.

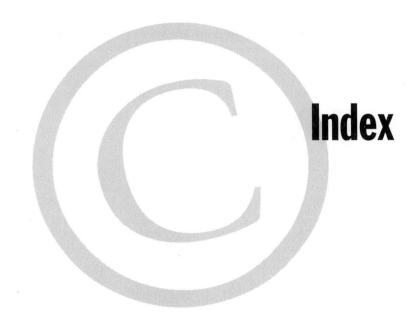

Index

and the Internet, 124
Convention for the Protection of Literary
and Artistic Works. *See* Berne
Convention.
copies
for copyright deposit, 68, 69, 168
and fixation, 17
glossary definition of, 165
and unpublished work, 179. *See also*
copying.
copying, 16, 17, 18, 21, 22, 28
of copyright registration forms, 67
of expression, 80, 91
and fair use, 85, 88
glossary definition of, 165
and infringement, 78–79, 80, 82, 90,
101, 165–66
and the Internet, 122–23
and originality, 172–73
of proposal(s), 40, 44
as a right, 169
in work-made-for-hire agreement,
159(n14)
Copyright Act of 1909, 50, 57
Copyright Act of 1976, 50, 57, 86, 127, 130
Copyright Office, U.S. Library of Congress,
14, 25, 29, 30, 34, 47, 51, 52, 53,
57, 63, 64, 65, 66, 67, 68, 69, 70,
71, 72, 73, 75, 114, 115, 146(n9),
164, 166, 168, 176
Copyright Office publications, 72–75
Copyright Protection Act, NII, 122
Copyright Renewal Act of 1992, 55
copyright treaties, 28, 31–32, 33, 34
creation, glossary definition of, 167
creator(s), of a work
as author, 162
and copyright transfer, 127, 157(n2)
as independent contractor, 170–71
and infringement, 83
rights of, 10, 77
of work made for hire, 53–54
See also author(s); freelancer(s);
independent contractor(s);

owner(s), copyright; work made
for hire.
cyberspace, and copyright, 120–25

D

damages, 100, 164, 171–72, 174, 176
actual, 69–70, 84, 161
statutory, 69–70, 161, 177
dance. *See* choreographic work(s).
data, research, 20
database, form to register, 65
defendant
glossary definition of, 167
in infringement cases, 16, 84, 89,
102–3, 167–68
defenses, glossary definition of, 167–68.
See also fair use.
Denmark, 25
deposit
copies, glossary definition of, 168
of copies for registration, 65, 68, 71
and trade secrets, 46–47
derivative work, 10, 27, 168, 169
design(s), 15, 20, 21, 179
design patent, 15, 173. *See also* patent(s).
diagrams, form to register, 65
diary, and term of copyright, 56
digital copying, 122–23. *See also* copying.
directories, 124
form to register, 65
disclosure, of trade secrets, 37, 38, 46. *See
also* non-disclosure letter.
discoveries, and copyright, 18, 19, 80, 169
discovery, in copyright litigation, 101
display, of copyrighted work, 168, 169, 175.
See also publication (verb).
document(s), and copyright, 8
dramatic work(s), 10, 49, 66
form to register, 65, 166
drawing(s), 17, 180
form to register, 65
duration, of copyright. *See* term of
copyright.

Allworth Books